# Financial Management for Technology Start-ups

## A handbook for growth

Alnoor Bhimani

**Publisher's note**

Every possible effort has been made to ensure that the information contained in this book is accurate at the time of going to press, and the publisher and author cannot accept responsibility for any errors or omissions, however caused. No responsibility for loss or damage occasioned to any person acting, or refraining from action, as a result of the material in this publication can be accepted by the editor, the publisher or the author.

First published in Great Britain and the United States in 2017 by Kogan Page Limited



2nd Floor, 45 Gee Street
London EC1V 3RS
United Kingdom
www.koganpage.com

c/o Martin P Hill Consulting
122 W 27th St,10th Floor
New York NY 10001
USA

4737/23 Ansari Road
Daryaganj
New Delhi 110002
India



ISBN 978 0 7494 8134 6
E-ISBN 978 0 7494 8135 3

**British Library Cataloguing-in-Publication Data**

A CIP record for this book is available from the British Library.

**Library of Congress Cataloging-in-Publication Data**

Names: Bhimani, Alnoor, author.
Title: Financial management for technology start-ups : a handbook for growth / Alnoor Bhimani.
Description: 1st Edition. | New York : Kogan Page Ltd, [2017] | Includes bibliographical references and index.
Identifiers: LCCN 2017023246 (print) | LCCN 2017030602 (ebook) | ISBN 9780749481353 (ebook) | ISBN 9780749481346 (alk. paper) | ISBN 9780749481353 (eISBN)
Subjects: LCSH: High technology industries–Finance. | New business enterprises–Finance.
Classification: LCC HG4027.6 (ebook) | LCC HG4027.6 .B52 2017 (print) | DDC 658.15–dc23

Typeset by Integra Software Services, Pondicherry
Print production managed by Jellyfish
Printed and bound in Great Britain by CPI Group (UK) Ltd, Croydon, CR0 4YY

# Praise for *Financial Management for Technology Start-ups*

"Mandatory reading for tech investors and entrepreneurs. Packed with straightforward illustrations and principles that blend finance into innovative business models. A smart, jargonless book that shows how accounting numbers can be used to propel a tech start-up to success." **Srikant M Datar, Arthur Lowes Dickinson Professor of Business Administration, Harvard Business School, and Faculty Chair, Harvard Innovation Lab, Harvard University, USA**

"Having a clear but flexible financial strategy is critical to a successful start-up. This guide is a must-read for any aspiring entrepreneur." **Lance Uggla, Chairman and Chief Executive, IHS Markit, UK**

"A great resource for founders looking to understand the key financial measures that impact their businesses, with many worked examples and cases directly relevant to the real challenges start-ups face. An essential addition to any founder's toolkit." **Kamran Malik, Partner, EY, UK**

"If you are involved in early-stage technology firms, be it as an entrepreneur, mentor or investor, this book will give you the financial management angle required to sustainably support and scale your start-up. It offers in a focused and persuasive manner what entrepreneurs need to know and investors want to know about tech start-ups." **Claudia Zeisberger, Professor, and Director, Global Private Equity Initiative, INSEAD**

"Tech start-ups are distinct from traditional companies ...they operate with fewer resources and in environments with more uncertainty, creating higher returns for certain activities such as continuous experimentation. Thus, specific skills are required to compete effectively – including start-up-oriented financial management. Al Bhimani has written the best text yet on this topic: concise and pragmatic. The book is a must-read." **Ajay Agrawal, Founder, Creative Destruction Lab, Cofounder, The Next 36, and Peter Munk Professor of Entrepreneurship, University of Toronto, Canada**

"Almost impossible to stop reading! This book for tech start-ups fills a big void. It will put the power of financial management at your fingertips in a way that's never been done before." **Mthuli Ncube, Professor, University of Oxford, UK, and Head, Quantum Global Research Lab, Switzerland**

"One of the biggest obstructions for tech start-ups reaching out to investors is lack of financial savvy. Now that obstacle is removed. This hands-on manual shows how to extract financial returns from tech innovations." **Jussi Siitonen, Chief Financial Officer, Amer Sports, Finland**

"Al Bhimani provides a practical and ready-to-use roadmap for tech entrepreneurs to build their ideas and grow their new ventures with solid financial strategy and management. ...this guide will support big ideas and life-changing innovations by allowing entrepreneurs to establish strong foundations, accelerate growth and create value." **Kerry Healey, President, Babson College, USA**

"The coolest book for the next generation of technology start-ups! Al Bhimani totally demystifies accounting to show how value can be unleashed from innovation. He does this by jettisoning long-held beliefs about finance and strategy." **Leif Sjoblom, Professor of Financial Management, IMD, Switzerland**

"Start-ups are chances to realize ambitions and reshape the world, but their success depends on more than good ideas. Effective financial management is crucial. Al Bhimani offers state-of-the-art guidance to entrepreneurs who need to know how each stage of business growth works, what to expect of financial professionals, and what questions to ask potential funders and partners." **Craig Calhoun, President, Berggruen Institute, USA**

"This elegant book deals with important issues missing from standard finance texts. A really useful guide for tech innovators looking to experience sustained growth." **Joshua Yindenaba Abor, Professor of Finance, and Dean of the University of Ghana Business School, Ghana**

"The only accounting book that will grip you until the end! This guide is indispensable for techpreneurs and tech investors in a hurry. It zeroes in on all the strategic financial insight tech start-ups hungry for growth require." **Antonio Dávila, Professor of Entrepreneurship and Accounting, IESE Business School, Spain**

"I wish this book had been written earlier... from founding my start-up through to IPO this would have been my finance bible." **Agam Jain, Founding Director, Jayex.com, Australia**

"An invaluable resource on the essentials of financial management for established and aspiring entrepreneurs alike." **Mark Maloney, Director of LSE Careers, UK**

"Bhimani's book covers what start-ups need to become profitable and get funded. The book is clear, concise, and easy to understand." **Hanno Roberts, Professor, Norwegian Business School, Norway**

"This is a groundbreaking book full of rich ideas that will benefit all entrepreneurs – Chinese and worldwide. No digital start-up can afford to ignore this book. With this book you succeed. Without it you will struggle." **Guliang Tang, Dean of the Business School, University of International Business and Economics, Beijing, China**

"A profoundly useful book on the financial management of tech start-ups. Essential reading for entrepreneurs." **Habib Mahama, Professor and Chair of the Accounting Department, UAE University College of Business and Economics, UAE**

"An excellent finance primer for high-tech entrepreneurs. It explains the fundamentals simply and coherently in a totally new way. The book connects finance insights with practical examples so entrepreneurs can make financial decisions and take action to grow the value of their ventures." **Azzim Gulamhussen, Professor of Banking and Finance, Vlerick Business School, Belgium**

"Far too many brilliant technological innovations have crashed – burned by the hubris that they did not need financial management competence. Bhimani guides his reader through the essentials of finance without which entrepreneurs cannot smell sweet success." **Shyam Sunder, James L Frank Professor of Accounting, Economics, and Finance, Yale University School of Management, USA**

"Tech start-ups need more than a great idea – they also need enough financial savvy to succeed. If you are about to launch a tech start-up, this book is essential reading." **Michael D Myers, Professor of Information Systems, University of Auckland Business School, New Zealand**

"This is the book entrepreneurs and investors have been waiting for. As cofounder of the Lisbon entrepreneurship centre, AUDAX, as well as the Building Global Innovators accelerator, I wish the many start-ups we supported had had this toolkit for financial management and valuation during their most sensitive early start-up stage." **José Paulo Esperança, Dean and Professor of Finance, ISCTE Business School, Portugal**

"Tech start-ups with extreme promise often fail to evolve due to weak financial grasp. This book rolls accounting, technology and business parameters into a complete single compass that will give tech entrepreneurs a rare edge." **Salvador Carmona, Professor, and Rector, IE University, Spain**

"This excellent book will equip tech entrepreneurs with all the financial knowledge they need in a simple and easy-to-digest manner that no other book offers." **Teemu Malmi, Professor and Head of Healthcare Productivity Research Group, Aalto University, Finland**

"A must-read for practitioners and academicians... this book offers a much-needed financial management perspective for leading and growing tech start-ups." **Jawad Syed, Dean and Professor of Organizational Behaviour, Suleman Dawood School of Business, Lahore University of Management Sciences, Pakistan**

"Al Bhimani has put together an extremely useful handbook for managing and growing tech start-ups. His clear description of the fundamentals will be very helpful to tech entrepreneurs." **Naomi Soderstrom, Professor of Accounting and Deputy Head of Department, University of Melbourne, Australia**

"As Al Bhimani states in this excellent book, 'tech start-ups are a different world'. But to succeed in this different world, one needs the financial and managerial know-how to make it happen, and this is what Bhimani provides. In this short, yet exhaustive and clearly written practical guide, start-up tech entrepreneurs will learn what they need to know about how to create value in their sector and how to monetize it." **Saul Estrin, Professor of Management and Founding Head of the Department of Management, London School of Economics, UK**

"This is a must-read! Thank you Al Bhimani for this book. It will oil tech start-up financial decisions and steer their strategic actions like no other can." **George Njenga, Dean, Strathmore Business School, Kenya**

"In the digital economy there can be unlimited technical solutions but very few financial options. So tech start-ups require a new type of accounting and finance from idea to execution. Using highly readable language, Professor Bhimani's practical book shows entrepreneurs how to harness financials and how to see their business through the eyes of investors." **Sergio Beretta, Professor, Bocconi University, Italy**

"Al Bhimani's book is an innovation. It rewrites the rules of finance for tech entrepreneurs who want to fire up their start-up's growth and shows how to meet every investor demand." **Fábio Frezatti, Professor, University of São Paulo, Brazil**

"This is a must-read for technology entrepreneurs, who will get a detailed understanding of how to assess their start-up's financial situation." **Sophie Manigart, Gimv Private Equity Chair, Vlerick Business School, and Professor, Ghent University, Belgium**

# CONTENTS

# ABOUT THE AUTHOR

Alnoor Bhimani is Founding Director of LSE Entrepreneurship and Professor of Management Accounting at the London School of Economics. He is interested in strategic finance, tech entrepreneurship, business growth and digital technologies.

# PREFACE

When we see a technological disruption in our world, it's because someone unleashed it. Somebody knew that it would change things, even before it started to transform how we perceive, think, do, experience or interact. Having a 'lightbulb moment' about a technological possibility isn't enough though. Only proper execution can make change happen. Coming up with an idea is the easy part – but mobilizing a real shift takes intelligent effort and action. This book will equip you with the financial intelligence you'll need to power a tech start-up. To launch and grow a tech business, you need an agile understanding of how it's going to create value, and the steps you need to take to monetize that value. Plenty of books and courses on financial management and accounting give you generic knowledge about finance. Then, you're left on your own to figure out how to apply this to a tech start-up. What those books and courses leave out is the precise financial savvy you need to apply to a start-up, where the focus is on technology and innovation. *This book homes in on lean, ready-to-use accounting and financial know-how specific to tech start-ups.* It will enable you to successfully drive your tech business model and to swiftly pinpoint emerging profit pathways. It will also help you determine how to raise finance and communicate with investors. By blending financial management principles into core tech business fundamentals, this book gives you the ultimate financial lens for tech start-up success.

Is now the best time for a tech start-up? Entrepreneurs don't wait for the best time. But right now, we're seeing probably the biggest technology-based transformational shift in the history of the world. This makes now the absolute perfect moment for tech entrepreneurs to act. And clearly, technological innovations wait for no one, so time windows for acting shut down fast. You'll need to understand the financial underpinnings of your tech start-up quickly. Many in the tech entrepreneurial ecosystem have pointed out the need to filter our knowledge of accounting and finance, to extract the parts that are relevant to technology and start-ups. This book does exactly that, in a form that you can understand fast and apply right away.

Will you benefit from this book? Tech start-ups that drive innovations using digital technologies are constantly evolving, finding more diverse ways to create value, to lower input costs and to broaden commercial applications. All these issues are addressed here. If you're one of almost two million people across the globe this year who will launch a business centred on a digital or technological innovation, then this book will be an essential resource for you. Equally, you'll want to read it if you're a policy-maker, social enterprise advocate, business angel or venture capitalist who needs to grasp the financial fundamentals of tech start-ups. If you're a student or teacher linked to university-based start-up and innovation labs, or involved in tech entrepreneurship courses requiring a focus on finance and accounting, you'll discover the material you need here. Further, incubators, accelerators, public and private institutions that promote tech start-ups, and corporate intrapreneurship initiatives will all regard what is covered in the book as vital to their work.

The approach in this book is *highly practical* with a focus on hands-on financial management practices linked to tech firms. We'll discuss specific cost issues and finance fundamentals in real-life form that are applicable to tech start-ups so that readers can use this knowledge directly. We'll also look at the financials of publicly-traded companies like Amazon, Facebook, eBay and others. Naturally, there is rigour in the material because of the emphasis on practical illustrations but what is conveyed has been pruned and cropped to bring out the absolute essentials. You'll find it easy to digest, so you can hit the ground running with financial management knowledge that's directly useful to tech start-ups. There'll be plenty of illustrations of the financials that underpin value creation for emerging tech innovations, such as mobile apps, big data, business analytics, the internet of things, blockchains and 3-D printing, among others. The last chapter of the book brings together metrics and key business performance drivers, in a 'Tech Start-up Tracker'. This is a scorecard tool that will help you monitor your start-up's progress, and provides pointers for making shifts in your operations or business hypothesis.

Because the book gives you a highly specific financial management lens through which to lead and grow tech start-ups, the book is not for you if you're an accountancy student looking to pass professional exams. It doesn't go into the specifics of double-entry bookkeeping or detailed accounting processes and standards, or tax issues. Neither will this book suit traditional companies looking for conventional managerial accounting and finance tools.

As you read this book, you'll learn about the sheer variety of business models which technology has unleashed. You'll see that networks, connections and the many channels of exchange specific to tech firms are at the root of value creation. You'll discover how the continuous experimentations around tech start-up activities need a special type of financial management attention. The book will explore the impact of externalizing activities and insourcing, and the differences between exploiting demand-side value effects as opposed to lowering costs on the supply side to grow your profits. We'll find that tried-and-tested corporate strategies for business success have just one useful role in the tech start-up economy – and that is to guide contrarian action! You'll see through many illustrations, over and over again, that financial management now has to reflect tech business realities:

- ✔ Clicks are costless.
- ✔ Systems don't need to be purchased.
- ✔ Initially, growth can come before profits.
- ✔ Increased sales don't have to be tied to rising costs.
- ✔ Tech can redirect gains from incumbent businesses to users and start-ups.

And you'll learn about tech start-up financial inversion where:

- ✔ Consumers and entrepreneurial savvy create value – not invested capital.
- ✔ Marginal costs are near zero and fixed costs can be made variable.
- ✔ Putting volume before profits can attract investors.
- ✔ Costs rise mathematically while value grows exponentially.
- ✔ Large tech players unlock a wave of new smaller incumbents.
- ✔ The service user doesn't need charging to trigger big start-up payoffs.

Chapters will explain, in detail, specific accounting fundamentals that you'll need. So you'll learn about:

- ✔ Costs that change and those that don't.
- ✔ The structure of an income statement and the balance sheet.
- ✔ The ultimate tool: contribution margin.
- ✔ Using budgets to project future profits.
- ✔ Lean accounting and driving growth through metrics.
- ✔ Using the right accounting pitch and financial ratios to investors.
- ✔ Monitoring financials to pinpoint profit growth sources.

Plus, you'll explore how you can:

- ✔ Cost your products and analyse variances.
- ✔ Use activity accounting to help your start-up maximize profits.
- ✔ Monitor customer acquisition costs, lifetime customer value and churn rate.
- ✔ Align your business goals to your investors' ROI target.
- ✔ Deploy the Tech Start-up Tracker to ensure you're heading in the right direction.

You'll already know that tech start-up founders are the rainmakers who find solutions to existing problems and develop products and services that enhance the way we live. The book presents all the financial intelligence needed to support this. Your tech start-up's growth journey begins here.

# LIST OF ABBREVIATIONS

| | |
|---|---|
| ATV | Average transaction value |
| B2B | Business-to-business |
| B2C | Business-to-consumer |
| C2C | Customer-to-customer |
| CAC | Customer acquisition cost |
| CCR | Customer churn rate |
| CD | Certificate of deposit |
| DPS | Dividend per share |
| EPS | Earnings per share |
| GAAP | Generally accepted accounting principles |
| IFRS | International financial reporting standards |
| IPO | Initial public offering |
| IRR | Internal rate of return |
| JOBS (Act) | Jumpstart our business start-ups |
| KPI | Key performance indicator |
| LTV | Lifetime value |
| MRR | Monthly recurring revenue |
| P2P | Peer-to-peer |
| ROA | Return on assets |
| ROI | Return on investment |
| ROE | Return on equity |
| SAFE | Simple agreement for equity |

# ACKNOWLEDGEMENTS

Many people have helped write this book. At Kogan Page, Melody Dawes immediately saw the merit of *Financial Management for Technology Start-ups* and her team provided much insight on structuring the book's content. Zoe Gilbert's editorial work has been invaluable. Brenda Clarkson-Williams, Mariam Faiz, Katherine Hartle, Susan Hodgson, Philippa Fiszzon and reviewers Antonio Malfense Fierro and Colin Barrow all provided valuable input.

I am thankful to the many who supported and helped create the LSE Entrepreneurship unit, which made evident the need for a book in this area. Countless participants who attended the talks, networking events, incubator activities, start-up workshops, entrepreneurship debates, funding competitions and policy briefs all, in one way or another, contributed to the ideas expressed here. A few that should be named are Zoltan Acs, Max Cartellieri, Duncan Clark, Eric Ries, Mo Ibrahim, Rohan Silva, Wol Kolade, Sherry Coutu, Kamran Malik, Daniela Papi-Thornton, Muhammad Yunus, Saul Estrin, Stelios Haji-Ioannou, Peter Thiel, Lance Uggla, Lisa Bridgett, David Stringer-Lamarre, Craig Calhoun, Susan Liautaud, Firoz Lalji, Mthuli Ncube, Kerry Healey and Adrian Wooldridge.

I thank my daughters Lia and Sofiya and my partner Farah for being there.

*For Farah*

# Now is the time 01

Almost daily, we see the launch of new tech start-ups that focus on technological innovations. But while all tech start-ups begin with a good idea, this in itself isn't enough. The business of technology is about much more than just an idea around the technology: what matters is the intelligent implementation of your idea. This book gives you the financial intelligence you need to manoeuvre your tech start-up, through both its launch and its growth. Why now? We find ourselves today at the start of another industrial revolution – and it would be hard to imagine more perfect conditions for launching a tech business. The first revolution happened 250 years ago, and depended on mechanization. The second, about a hundred years ago, was all about electrification and mass production. Electronics and automation started a third revolution around 50 years ago. Right now, we're witnessing a fourth revolution, as our physical and virtual worlds converge. This is changing the way we produce, consume, move, communicate and interact. With the first three revolutions, not many people knew the scale of the changes taking place. *The difference today is that we know we're entering a transformation* that is epochal, and we also know we can influence its direction. It's this new awareness which makes now the best possible time to launch and grow a tech start-up.

Some tech start-ups have become big businesses in a short time: companies like Alphabet, Facebook and Amazon have created massive value for their users, producers and customers. But unlike large industrial companies such as Volkswagen, China National Petroleum, Foxconn and Walmart, such colossal tech giants have also allowed lots of new businesses to be born – some big and some small. Consequently, there are many ways to make money in the digital economy. Anyone can now combine Google's capacity to provide unbounded information with access to almost one-quarter of the globe's population via Facebook. Add to that the ready availability of cheap, or even free, ices, and you can be on your way to creating a tech busi- ılso now straightforward to develop ad content and get it in eaders, via Google AdSense or Amazon Affiliate, for example. So there's little to stop someone with an idea and some drive from launching a tech start-up. A galaxy of opportunities is opening up through engaging with technology commercially – and some start-ups launching right now will become the tech titans of tomorrow.

Every day, we see how technologies push forward the boundaries of automation and digitization, and these in turn make for increases in productivity, efficiency, exchange and enjoyment. We see how technologies alter when, where, why and how we do things. As the fourth industrial revolution takes hold, there'll be ever more entwining of the material and the digital, and this will offer huge possibilities for reconfiguring our activities and exchanges. The first key thing to understand though is what's different about tech businesses, meaning they need a particular approach to financial management. So, in this chapter we'll think about:

- whether financial management is all that essential;
- how tech business models are re-inventing business;
- why a different sort of financial intelligence is needed;
- how the financial management lens presented in this book will power your start-up's growth.

## Why bother with financial management?

Time is always short, and learning about financial management means you're taking valuable time away from your start-up – is it at all worthwhile? Successful entrepreneurs, business school professors and business commentators will say you really need to learn some accounting and finance if your start-up is to succeed. They'll tell you that this knowledge will serve you in a number of ways. First, you want to be able to work out if you're getting more out of your business activities than you're putting in. In other words, *are you creating value*? To do this, you'll need to know how to keep track of what your customers are giving you, compared to what you've put in. So, you'll have to know something about costs and revenues, and once you do, you'll be able to work out the economic contribution your business makes.

Second, if you know you're creating value, you'll then also need to work out if you're where you should be. And knowing where you should be means having some forecasts and predictions which crystallize your aims. So, if you're targeting where you want to be at a future point and you carry out activities in that direction, you'll want to be able to track, at any time, whether you're achieving what you're aiming for. The question will be: *are you creating as much value as you set out to?*

Third, you'll also want to gauge whether you're working smart. That's really asking: *are you using the fewest resources you can to generate the most value possible?* So you'll need to know a bit about the assets you've got and the value you're getting out of them. If you're working really smart, you'll be making a huge contribution but using up few resources.

Finally, if you've got the potential to create a huge amount of value because of your ideas, skills and energy but don't have the cash to make this happen, you'll want to get your hands on someone else's money! If they're going to give you any money though, they'll have high expectations. Investors in start-ups are aware that more than one-third of business failures are due to founders having a poor understanding of financial management (ACCA, 2016). In the US, half of small businesses fail within a year and almost 90 per cent of business failures are due to management mistakes, including a lack of financial responsibility and awareness (Titus, 2017). Inadequate financial understanding is seen as a key reason for start-up failure across Europe (European Union, 2016), the Middle East and North Africa (*Economist*, 2017) and other countries like India (Imorphosis, 2016), China (Liu, 2016), Australia (Swan, 2015), Malaysia (Rahman *et al*, 2016) and Brazil (Cheston, 2016). So, investors will set targets for you and they'll want financial information about your start-up's progress. They'll need to know: *have you really got enough financial savvy to run a tech start-up?*

All these are true reasons why you need to be financially literate. But you already know that financial management awareness will help your start-up better communicate with investors, implement business strategies and swiftly pinpoint emerging pathways for profit. That's why you're reading this book. The bigger question, then, is this: is the new business of tech start-ups so different that it needs a unique approach to accounting and finance? We'll see below that the answer is, overwhelmingly, yes. This is the real reason why you should be reading this book. Let's explore some specific tech business models and then see what makes the financial know-how you need so different.

## The new business of business

Any business venture needs to be founded on a **business model**. This represents the premise on which the business will create and deliver value. For a commercial company, this means identifying how it will make money, what the customer base will be for its products and how it will finance itself. Of course, in this book we're focusing on **tech start-ups**. That's a company which will either deliver technology-based products and services in a new way, or create new and innovative technology-based solutions. Technology encompasses both software and hardware – you might for instance be developing an app (software) or a smarter smart tablet (hardware), or some combination of the two. Your tech start-up could be trying to sell products or services to other companies (**business-to-business** or **B2B**) or it could sell directly to individuals (**business-to-consumer** or **B2C**). Or perhaps, it could be facilitating exchanges or transactions of products and services between consumers (**customer-to-customer** or **C2C**). Your tech venture could be a **hard science** start-up, which uses technology to advance solutions in, say, material science, age-related health decline, genome challenges, robotics, and so on. It could be operating in the **deep tech** sector, which includes big data, machine learning and artificial intelligence. Or, it may be a **fintech** business that delivers financial services by making use of software and modern technology. It could be premised to some degree on creating a **platform**, with the aim of enabling interactions between users, producers and consumers. Established tech firms may have a wide range of product offerings, and use platform innovation to differing extents (see Moazed and Johnson, 2016; Parker *et al*, 2016). Firms like Apple, Amazon, Tencent, PayPal, Flipkart, Snapchat, Mercado Livre, Facebook, Baidu, Alphabet, Rakuten, eDreams, Zalando, Cimpress and Asos are all platform businesses. They give users the means to connect and interact on a spectacular scale, but also in different ways.

In the tech world, there is no set way of doing things. In fact, at the heart of technological change lies disruption. Start-ups experiment with different ways of using technology, usually to come up with new forms of benefit for consumers. Business models in tech firms may hinge on better quality of supply, more transparent service, lower prices, new ways of bundling services and often, entirely new drivers of value that will create their own further market needs. *Tech business is always about making a difference while creating value.* So, how do tech business models achieve this? Let's explore some key ones and then discuss why they need a different type of accounting.

One tech business model is the **freemium** model. This is where users get a variety of features free of charge, which means the company can develop an initial broad base of customers. Once the customer likes the broad offering, the company can sell them additional elements, with users choosing different services for small payments. Examples of firms using the freemium model are Xing, Dropbox, Skype and LinkedIn. Another model is the **advertising business model**, where users are exposed to adverts that represent a major source of money for these companies. Google and Baidu, for instance, get users coming back to their site for free searches.

Another business model rests on **experience-oriented crowd users**. Central to this model is the user's emotional experience that is created when they access the platform. Here, the value created is outsourced to the public group of users, and then each individual user's contribution benefits other users. Typically, there are lots of monetization possibilities for these businesses through analysing their users' interactions and profiles. Examples are Facebook, Sina Weibo, Tune.pk, Twitter, YouKu, Pandora.tv or Niconico. Depending on who you ask and when, you will hear different opinions on the financial value captured by start-ups using this business model. Take the example of Snapchat a few years ago. FundersClub (2017) nicely recalls the story. In late 2012, Snapchat's (now Snap Inc) co-founders Evan Spiegel and Bobby Murphy were meeting Mark Zuckerberg (chairman, CEO and co-founder of Facebook). The meeting wasn't entirely amicable, with Zuckerberg being very clear about Facebook's newest product:

> Poke, a mobile app for sharing photos that automatically disappear a few seconds after they're viewed. According to Spiegel, the meeting essentially amounted to 'We will crush you'. Luckily for Snapchat, Poke ultimately flopped, and drove more Snapchat sign-ups in the process. Zuckerberg soon returned to Spiegel and Murphy, hat-in-hand, and singing a different tune: $3 billion for all Snapchat's business. For a company not yet generating any revenue and lacking a clear path to profitability, the offer seemed too good to be true. So, investors were shocked when Snapchat turned down the deal, and wondered whether the company would fizzle out without any cash flow. Over time, Spiegel proved that his instincts were right. The Snapchat valuation skyrocketed from $3 billion in 2012, to over $15 billion in March 2015.
>
> FundersClub, 2017

At its initial public offering on 1 March 2017, the company was valued at $33 billion. A tech business model can therefore produce huge value, but it's only when a financial transaction takes place that the exact value gets firmed up. Snapchat and Facebook, of course, are also advertising-driven business firms.

Then, there is the **subscriptions** business model. This model requires users to subscribe to the service, paying fixed fees periodically. Examples of firms using this approach include Spotify, Hooq, Adobe, IFlix and Netflix. A close cousin of this model is the **price-per-user** model, where one payment gives permanent access; iPhone apps or Microsoft Office are examples of this. The **e-commerce** or e-tailer business model, not surprisingly, sells products or services on the internet. The sales can be direct, without intermediaries, or indirect. Examples are Amazon, Alibaba, Rakuten and Flipkart. The **brokerage** model facilitates buying and selling, and charges a fee for transactions. This is used by the likes of eBay, Taobao and Mercari.

These platforms make buying and selling items very simple and naturally attract users with their own smartphones or devices enabling an almost infinite marketplace. The intense connectivity that such large tech firms make possible lets almost anyone reach out to a massive market audience for next to nothing. Then, there are **partnership** platforms, where companies get paid a commission for passing on customers to third-party service providers. And lastly, there's the pure **lead generator model**, where a business sells information about users to other companies. Examples of these include Idealo, MySmartPrice, Moneysupermarket and Pricetory, as well as Lawyers.com and Yourhearing.co.uk.

These models and other variants continue to emerge, all using web-based technologies to create value in new ways. Now, we'll explore why they need a different type of accounting and finance understanding – one that reflects their business model specifics and start-up priorities.

## Like never before

So, what are some of the things that are different about tech-based firms compared with conventional industrial businesses? And how does that alter the financial intelligence you need? Ten years ago, there was just one tech company ranked among the world's six most valuable companies: Microsoft. Today, five of the globe's six most valuable businesses are tech companies (Dogs of the Dow, 2017). Financial management hasn't changed much in the past decade, so it should come as no surprise that tech founders have had to learn the accounting used by those who ran old-economy industrial firms – and then customize it for the tech scene. While technology has advanced apace and business models have rapidly evolved, financial management techniques haven't kept up. Textbook-based accounting and finance today gives little insight into how different the business processes that power the digital economy really are. Yet innovations in technology have transformed the financial circuitry of tech businesses. So, what exactly is so different in today's tech firms that we should adopt a new financial lens for managing tech start-ups? Let's take a look.

First, today's tech firms don't amass resources under one roof. Instead, they work on *connections* and derive value from creating and managing **networks**. These networks are made up of producers, consumers and users of products, services and information. Lots of traditional industrial firms relied on producing in large quantities, making money through economies of scale. They could undercut smaller businesses by *focusing on the supply side of things*, like bulk-buying, to push down their material costs. They could then invest in faster and more flexible technologies. As their costs went down, their efficiencies rose, which is how they became profitable giants in their industrial sectors. With many tech firms, the *focus has moved to the demand side.* They use technological innovations to create and expand networks. The growth of networks becomes self-reinforcing, because users get value out of connections and so connections grow. The larger user base in the network increases demand for the product, which in turn fuels even more network expansion and demand. Sometimes, networks connect with other networks. When connections become multi-dimensional in this way, they can lead to yet more connections and create even more value. Aside from the focus on demand in tech firms, this focus on networks causes another fundamental change. Tech firms can break away from the traditional business focus on sequenced, linear value chains, where there's a specific set of steps to follow in the production, sale, delivery and consumption of the firm's output (see Parker *et al*, 2016 for an insightful discussion). Networks make connections and interactions possible without following a one-way path.

Why is this important to you? If business transactions grow because networks expand in many directions and defy linear pathways, then *there's no point using financial intelligence that only sees linear paths of value creation.* Networks of connections that are multi-dimensional won't make sense to this kind of narrow accounting! Traditional ways of visualizing financial flows are just fine for old industrial firms, where everything follows a sequence with just one entry point and one exit. That type of accounting insight could prove pretty constraining for your tech start-up. Your focus may well need to be on interactions across different routes, channels and structures. You'll want to be equipped to make fast and intelligent decisions in networked and connected environments. To properly advance your start-up, *you'll need light-speed accounting insight that reflects the new fundamentals of tech business*. You don't want to be held back by financial management meant for more conventional businesses. If you can't see where your tech business is creating value, you won't be able to manage it.

That's not to say that we should just jettison long-established accounting techniques and financial statements. In fact, in this book we'll learn quite a bit about key financial statements such as balance sheets, income statements, cash flow statements and budgets – all of which are very useful for capturing vital financial information. Bookkeeping and tax processes are important too, and you'll still need to use an accountant for your start-up to take care of these essential tasks, which are not going to be our focus in this book. You just need a lean, straightforward and focused financial lens that speaks directly to the new dimensions of tech business. What's vital to grasp here is that there's new financial plumbing underneath your tech business which you need to see through, so you're equipped to power the right kinds of decisions for your start-up.

Second, tech start-ups need to *continuously experiment* and try to innovate. They are not like traditional business ventures, where you work out the resources you need to serve a market segment for a product with established value. You won't have the comfort of such certainty – especially if your offering requires **product–market fit** testing and fine-tuning. Instead you might want to test out an altered product feature, toy with a new website feature angle, explore building relationships with influencers, try out a differentiated pricing scheme, play around with a mobile-responsive template, work out novel organic tactics to increase online traffic, and so on. Some of your experiments will have only tiny business repercussions, while others could unleash strategic-level changes. You might experiment with small aspects of the business model, to see how it could be stretched. Or, you may reach the point where you want to chuck out your whole business hypothesis and try out a new premise for generating value (Ries, 2011). And so, from a financial viewpoint, you'll need specific ways to track activities that help you determine what actions to take, and when, as your business evolves. Again, what's essential is that your accounting intelligence must help you manoeuvre your start-up in a very specific way, *through close tracking and monitoring of your experimental activities.*

A third reason for the difference is that tech firms tend to *externalize activities* that are costly. Many tech powerhouses like Apple, Samsung and Tesla invest in both traditional resources and online networks. Others, like Alphabet and Baidu, invest purely in the technology of connections. Consider Uber, where drivers use their own car, insurance, maintenance and smartphone. *The factors of production are essentially theirs* – it's their car, their labour, their time and their resources. Most drivers opt to use their own smartphone too, which they use to download the Uber app. These drivers just get connected to passengers. This is what you'd expect, since as a platform, Uber simply enables drivers and passengers to interface. Then when rides take place, it creates value for all parties: directly for the passengers, the driver and Uber, and indirectly for the tax authorities, mobile network operator, the car insurer and so on. Externalizing activities like this enables platforms to own much less than their competitors with industrial business models. Just as Uber doesn't own the vehicles passengers ride in, Alibaba doesn't have its own inventory of goods, and Airbnb doesn't own the accommodation its users occupy. Weibo likewise doesn't create content. When we translate this into accounting terms, it means tech businesses have high potential to bring in a lot of money, without owning physical resources or taking on costly labour activities.

The resources tech start-ups need to create and deliver solutions just aren't on the same level and scope as for less connected, conventional businesses. It's important to take this into account, because it *alters the amount of money your tech start-up will ask investors for.* Aside from externalizing resources, tech businesses can also use plug-and-play models. This allows them to create value chains straightaway, by linking up third-party products and services. A tech firm can '*insource*' (Pierides and Gosling, 2016) systems and seamlessly orchestrate the operations of other suppliers. For instance, Expedia enables flights, hotels and car rentals to be booked simultaneously, as well as providing insurance coverage and visa services. It does this by connecting providers and putting all this together into one packaged product for the customer. The real-time online aggregation of products and services in this way *pushes down overall costs*. This is because virtual connections make for lower transaction costs. A tech firm's ability to extend, change and reconfigure value chains means they can make profits much more efficiently than in the conventional business world. The firm gives users a broader array of options, and it can monetize the value of these, at some later stage. We need then to have a specific financial intelligence to understand the mechanics of reaching high returns once initial costs are covered. Ultimately, externalizing resources and insourcing other providers' facilities both directly affect a start-up's financing needs and its value-creation activities. So, you'll want to use an accounting approach that allows you to properly visualize the effects of both these elements on your start-up.

A fourth feature of tech businesses, that means they need a specific sort of financial management understanding, is that they can cause disruptions in existing industries. Take, for instance, services like providing accommodation for travellers (eg Wimdu.com) or hiring a bike from a cyclist who's got a spare (Spinlister.com). Here, the premise is that when your customer makes cash, you get a cut. Models associated with the **sharing economy** rely very specifically on new sources of value creation being brought into the market from existing supplies. So, these companies don't have to make investments into anything that's not already there. The tech platform simply enables users who need a service or product to come together with suppliers who have unused capacity, benefiting all parties. Traditional suppliers such as taxis, trains and other pre-existing transport services had to invest into new resources to bring to life their business model. But with tech start-ups in this business space, existing supply sources are unleashed bringing spare capacity onto the market. As a result of supply increasing, the traditional providers now have to share customer spend with the new suppliers. This brings down prices across the whole industry, as there's so much more supply. So, the *conventional providers' prior profits now get redistributed*. Some of this goes to the new suppliers of spare capacity, and some to the consumers who now have more choice with lower price points being available. Naturally, the business platform itself takes a slice of the created value: consumers in North America and Europe get upward of $280 billion worth of 'free' services from the web, that would have cost money or time (*Economist*, 2017).

Alongside the sharing economy, the **gig economy** is fast growing and founded on a similar business premise. It provides a way for people to work on temporary jobs and do separate pieces of work, that earn them an income independently of one another. Platforms such as Upwork.com connect job-seekers in IT areas to those who need them. Care.com puts together care workers with individuals who want care services. Dogvacay.com gets you a dog-sitter. The possibilities of such digital platforms extend from high-skilled/high-paid to low-skilled/low-paid workers and can be local or cross-national. There is thus huge potential for creating value from generating new work opportunities for people.

The data that start-ups in this space collect also offer value. These data can be useful in identifying new work trends and needs, and can point to new ways of extending services into other areas (for instance, a passenger transportation platform extending into parcel delivery, food delivery, etc). Some have suggested that the effects on society aren't always positive. Uber, which links people who want rides with drivers who provide travel at a fee, has faced much ire from regulators. But this, too, helps the start-up ecosystem: slight variations on Uber's business model to get past regulatory hurdles have launched very successfully. BlaBlaCar, for instance, developed a technology platform which, as Clifford (2015) notes, 'connects drivers and riders headed in the same direction and allows riders to pay drivers enough to cover reasonable expenses, like gas and automobile wear and tear. The ridesharing platform does not let drivers make a profit off of its passengers. BlaBlaCar makes money by collecting a transaction fee, approximately 10 per cent of the total cost of a ride.' So, we can see how the sharing or gig economy helps make use of spare capacity, creates opportunities for suppliers and a more differentiated, lower-cost market for users, while sponsoring new business models. Tech start-ups in this space need to use financial monitors and metrics to assess how the growth of the network evolves, and where consumer and supplier connections affect costs and generate profit. Tech business models can extend capacity in an industry, and force a re-jigging of the cash profits across many more market players. Understanding the mechanics of such models in a financially insightful manner is essential for any tech entrepreneur.

A fifth dimension that differentiates the financial intelligence that tech firms require is their capacity to *collect data*. Of course, all firms do this, converting it into usable information that can support good decision-making in search of creating more value. All companies use accounting information to make decisions about day-to-day activities, and about more consequential strategic changes. They have access to data on product sales, customer purchases, promotions impact, cash flows and so on, which they can harness as a source of value in their own respect.

User information which is aggregated can give useful pointers about customer behaviour, preferences and partialities. This provides firms with avenues for further economic value growth (*Economist*, 2016). Many tech businesses however have access to data from a wide variety of other sources, including ones that reflect connections and exchanges between individuals and also between people and things. This can derive from tools like product sensors and ID tags, for example, enabled by the ever-growing Internet of Things economy. Further, some tech business increase the flow of data and connectivity not just between people and things, but between things and things. This is something the old economy industries never did. And while products and services that customers access can sponsor company growth, *data itself can also provide extreme business expansion potential* for these firms.

Big data collection and analysis can give us predictive insights which traditional accounting information cannot tap. By convention, accounting information on a business's performance is based on the past – that is, historical records of transactions like sales, purchases and payments made. But access to data on a macro scale ahead of actual economic transactions enables all firms, especially ones using digital platforms, to gather more *data about predictive rather than historical transactions*. The ability to use this kind of data is what attracts many investors to tech start-ups. Accounting to assess the value of such data-led insights has become very relevant, and it requires financial analyses that weren't called for in traditional businesses.

So, we've covered a few good reasons why tech businesses need to treat financial management and accounting information differently from traditional, industrial firms. We'll see the insight you can unleash by looking through your start-up's business hypothesis and its progress through the eyes of the leaner financial management we cover in the chapters coming up. Doing this will accelerate your start-up's value creation without you having to learn any hard-core accountancy that is, in any case, going to be too narrow for your tech business. The journey to growing your start-up using a lean and tech-focused financial management lens is about to begin.

## Summary of chapter

We've reviewed why:

- your tech start-up needs you to apply financial management savvy;
- technology is enabling new business models;
- a different sort of financial intelligence is needed;
- lean financial management is essential to power your start-up's growth.

## Review questions

1. Why is the new industrial revolution offering such huge possibilities for tech start-ups?
2. Why is financial management necessary to manage any business?
3. What type of business model does your start-up rest on to create value?
4. Why must financial management know-how be different for tech start-ups today?
5. What aspect of your start-up likely alters the financial management circuitry you need to be able to visualize?

## Further reading

Afuah, A and Tucci, CL (2001) *Internet Business Models and Strategies*, McGraw Hill, New York

Brynjolfsson, E and McAfee, A (2016) *The Second Machine Age: Work, progress, and prosperity in a time of brilliant technologies*, WW Norton & Company, New York

EFI Report (2016) Business models of the digital economy, available from www.e-fi.de/fileadmin/Chapter_2016/2016_B3_EN.pdf [accessed 21.3.17]

Rifkin, J (2015) *The Zero Marginal Cost Society: The internet of things, the collaborative commons, and the eclipse of capitalism*, Palgrave Macmillan, New York

Rogers, DL (2016) *The Digital Transformation Playbook: Rethink your business for the digital age*, Columbia University Press, New York

Schwab, K (2016) *The Fourth Industrial Revolution*, World Economic Forum, Geneva, Switzerland

## References

ACCA (2016) NI entrepreneurs are missing vital financial skills to ensure the success of their business, available from www.accaglobal.com/uk/en/news/2016/july/ni-entrepreneurs-missing-vital-skills.html [accessed 21.3.17]

Cheston, S (2016) The business of financial inclusion: Insights from banks in emerging markets, Institute of International Finance, available from http://www.centerforfinancialinclusion.org/storage/documents/IIF_CFI_Report_FINAL.pdf [accessed 21.3.17]

Clifford, C (2015) How BlaBlaCar is different from Uber, 8 September 2015, available at www.entrepreneur.com/article/250420 [accessed 21.3.17]

Dogs of the Dow (2017) Largest companies by market cap today, available at dogsofthedow.com/largest-companies-by-market-cap.htm [accessed 21.3.17]

*Economist* (2016) The rise of the superstars (Special Report), 17 September 2016, available from www.economist.com/sites/default/files/20160917_companies.pdf [accessed 21.3.17]

*Economist* (2017) Start-ups in the Arab world, 14 January 2017, available from www.economist.com/news/middle-east-and-africa/21714335-arab-entrepreneurs-could-help-many-regions-problems-too-many [accessed 21.3.17]

European Union (2016) Europe's next leaders: the Start-up and Scale-up Initiative, available from https://ec.europa.eu/transparency/regdoc/rep/1/2016/EN/COM-2016-733-F1-EN-MAIN.PDF [accessed 21.3.17]

FundersClub (2017) Startup Business Model Examples, available at fundersclub.com/learn/guides/exploring-the-tech-startup-space/business-model-examples/ [accessed 21.3.17]

Imorphosis (2016) 9 Genuine reasons for failed startups in India, available from imorphosis.com/reasons-failed-startups-in-india/ [accessed 21.3.17]

Liu, MB (2016) A Study of the Market Failure in the Financing of High-Tech SMEs and the Governmental Intervention, *Open Journal of Social Sciences*, 4, 163–69, available from dx.doi.org/10.4236/jss.2016.43022 [accessed 21.3.17]

Moazed, A and Johnson, NL (2016) *Modern Monopolies: What it takes to dominate the 21st century economy*, St Martin's Press, New York

Parker, G, Van Alstyne, M and Choudary, SP (2016) *Platform Revolution: How networked markets are transforming the economy – and how to make them work for you*, WW Norton & Company, New York

Pierides, M and Gosling, C (2016) IT Insourcing: What do you need to know?, available from www.itproportal.com/2016/07/28/it-insourcing-what-do-you-need-to-know/ [accessed 21.3.17]

Rahman, NA, Yaacob, Z and Radzi, RM (2016) The Challenges Among Malaysian SMEs: A theoretical perspective, *World Journal of Social Sciences*, 6, 3, pp 124–32

Ries, E (2011) *The Lean Startup: How today's entrepreneurs use continuous innovation to create radically successful businesses,* Crown Business, New York

Swan, D (2015) Australian start-ups failing financial literacy test, available from www.theaustralian.com.au/business/business-spectator/australian-start-ups-failing-financial-literacy-test/news-story/b8c471ff3143b41821293efd1dc82433 [accessed 21.3.17]

Titus, S (2017) Key reasons why small businesses fail, available from www.summitbusinesssolutions.ws/docs/reasons_biz_fail.pdf [accessed 21.3.17]

# Tech start-ups: It's a different world

02

This book is based on the idea that tech start-ups are so different from industrial firms that we need a completely different way of thinking about their financial management. But what is so different about managing tech start-ups? In this chapter, we'll look at the key ideas which have guided firms effectively in the 20th century, and the thinking behind strategies for corporate growth. But tech start-ups operate in a totally different world, with different ways to create value and disperse that value: this changes everything. We'll see how applying traditional managerial wisdom to a start-up can thwart its success, but we'll also learn from this: seeing tech businesses through a traditional lens can enable useful *contrarian* action. Then, we'll look at how the most fundamental premise of business financing – the risk–return dynamic – differs for tech businesses. By the end of this chapter, you'll know just how different things are for tech firms, and you'll be all set to explore the kind of financial plumbing you won't want to do without to grow your tech start-up. So, this chapter will look at:

- the idea of continuous feedback loops of information;
- why tech start-up founders need to be contrarian strategists;
- key dimensions of costs and volume effects;
- novel ways of generating tech-based value;
- why risk–return elements influence funding strategies and managing finances.

## Growth in a tech world

Over the past 40 years, firms have relied on certain business fundamentals to manage opportunities, as well as turbulence along the way. If we applied these old models to a new start-up, they might well help us, just not in the way we'd expect. By seeing the limits of old paradigms, we'll understand the scale of new possibilities, as well as the new methods we're going to need! If you wanted to launch a conventional business, you'd want to take a close look at the market for your product or service, and think about the costs involved. You'd assess your competition, the supplier chains and other factors that might affect the business opportunity, and you'd think about how you could add value. You'd look to do better than other providers, take account of product substitutes, and be clear on the risks and challenges facing you. And of course, you'd look at how much funding you'd need to start the business. This would involve a business plan, checking the resources needed, and giving potential investors some solid projections of cash inflows and outflows.

Basically, you'd follow pretty much the same sequence as every other new business launch in the industry. Once the business was up and running, you'd assess customer sales and expenses. If you found problems or new opportunities, you'd need to respond in a way that would both benefit investors and seem sensible to managers. This means that tried and tested ways of getting a new business going, making it viable, expanding and achieving profits, can be applied over and over again in the same way. And you'd be ok to rely on the savvy of managers who have seen it all before, as well as looking at case studies of other businesses in the industry. So, a conventional business start-up would stick to traditional managerial folklore, because it's known to work.

But tech start-ups are radically different. The linear logic of traditional small business management doesn't apply to them very well. As we saw in Chapter 1, tech firms and in particular, those that are platform-focused, defy the old industrial business focus on value chains that follow a linear sequence along a one-dimensional flow-path of production, sale, delivery and consumption activities. Tech start-ups tend to be founded by a team of people who each bring their own skill set. As a founder, you'd test the market differently at the initial stage. To get going without a proven idea, or an assured market, you'd want to get particular services at low cost that will quickly support your running needs. You might look to open-source software and some pay-as-you go services. These are so cheap initially that you'd only have to use up limited resources to try out your product idea, and see if it has traction. You could use cloud computing (perhaps through Amazon Web Services (AWS), Microsoft Azure or Google Cloud) to get infinite computer power and storage, without much planning or initial investment in your IT. Cloud-based services are attractive because they offer hosting possibilities, data centre infrastructure and system support – all the basic building blocks to get started and grow. Some successful start-ups like Spotify, Shazam and Hailo began this way. Others, once they grow, build their own data centres to serve more specific needs. Unlike traditional businesses, tech start-ups operate within *continuous feedback loops* where control, action and decision become woven together. Ongoing experimentation becomes vital to move a start-up forward. You need mechanisms for reacting to new information to keep the start-up on a positive course. This information should tell you when to make small changes to the experiments you're doing. It will also tell you when to **pivot** (Ries, 2011) the business, and make fundamental changes. Sometimes these changes mean revising the business hypothesis that your whole business plan was founded on.

Your start-up will develop a product and test it on customers, or even pay people to try it out. This way you can develop different configurations, adjusting and fine-tuning the product to better meet, or indeed create, user need. As you get this information about the product and how customers are using it, you need to analyse it. Then, any learning must translate into developing the product further, until you reach some level of *product–market engagement*. If you find you're getting signals that the start-up could scale up successfully, and become a larger market force, then you'll need funding. And you might need it very fast, depending on the market opportunity and how your product is changing or creating user needs. If your business is based on disrupting the usual ways that consumer needs are met, then the variables at play may need unusual financial analysis. A disruptive start-up like this may create a range of ripple effects that haven't been witnessed before, so you can't compare them with past experience. In effect, the usual sequential and linear logic you'd use to manage more conventional start-ups is often, by necessity, alien to tech start-ups.

It's not just the management decision-making within a tech start-up that's going to need different financial management tools. The forces unleashed by new technologies can trigger a load of different consequences and parameters. These might relate to connections between customers, consumers and products. There may be market creation, size, location and transformation issues to take account of. They can alter the whole basis for financial management of your start-up. So, you have to think differently about your underlying management strategy, too. We'll see in Chapter 3 that the cost structure of tech firms is not the same as for other businesses. Tech firms have to consider the way costs behave. Otherwise they might miss important cues for progressing the start-up that come via continuous loops of feedback information, which might then lead to missing action cycles. For now, though, it's worth remembering that conventional business thinking can still be useful for us to consider. It gives us a rationale for why we should tackle a start-up's business challenges differently, and can be a lens for looking at tech-based business.

## Reaching for stars

Let's start by looking at one of the most successful business thinking tools ever devised. The **growth share matrix** was developed by Bruce Henderson (1970), the founder of the Boston Consulting Group. As the *Financial Times* has noted: 'Few people have had as much impact on international business in the second half of the 20th century'. The matrix takes market growth and market share as two dimensions that have an impact on a company's products or business units. It helps us work out how to deal with limited resources. The matrix is shown in Figure 2.1.

The matrix suggests that 'dogs', which operate in the low market share/low growth quadrant, don't produce cash and probably don't need cash. They might be negative profitability products which we

**Figure 2.1** The growth share matrix

| | | Market Share | |
|---|---|---|---|
| | | High | Low |
| Market Growth | High | *STAR* | *WILDCAT* |
| | Low | *CASH COW* | *DOG* |

**SOURCE** Adapted from Henderson (1970)

should really get rid of, unless we're sure we can rethink their value or rebrand them. The common route is to eliminate dogs. A 'wildcat' (also referred to as a 'question mark' or 'problem child') product could be very innovative, and operate in a space with high market growth. But, it will need large investments if it's going to gain market share and eventually produce high returns. We need to make big decisions about whether the wildcat product is worth supporting. It will need cash resources, and it's such high risk that it might not be profitable in the end. 'Star' products are ones in the high market share/high growth corner. These are products that will need continuous investment in advertising and promotion, as well as upgrading, so they retain market allure. When we expect further market growth of this kind, we'll get aggressive competition from other companies in this space.

The real cash producers are the 'cash cows' in the high market share/low growth quadrant. They can generate a lot of cash because, while the market share is high, any new competitors are put off. They'd find it difficult to gain traction against market leaders who have already got brand recognition and production efficiencies. Also, since market growth is slowing, there's not much point in a new competitor trying to make inroads here. So, these products have high customer retention, low costs, and can be very profitable. But, if they're in a market that's quite mature, they're likely to be replaced. This could happen through product innovation, or simply because customer needs either disappear or are met through other product solutions. This growth share matrix is popular with multi-product companies, who use it to decide how to allocate resources. What pointers does it offer for tech start-ups?

We can think of a start-up as one of many investments funded by a business angel or venture capitalist, or as part of a large firm's intrapreneurial portfolio of business ventures. Some tech start-ups will in effect be in the dog quadrant, given the low market share/low growth space they have in their early stages. But, the product they're offering could show great promise for both market growth and share in the future. It's not clear that we should treat the start-up in the same way we'd treat a dog company in a traditional industrial sector context, where an investor would usually get rid of it. In fact, it might be better to invest resources in backing up a tech firm in this space, if the concept shows remote but positive signs of possible demand. This could be the case for asteroid mining, drone-based delivery systems or space travel tourism, for instance. Lots of companies have started by showing users a new form of value, only to then grow. These kinds of companies have also spawned hundreds of thousands of other start-ups, some of which have grown too, while others stayed small but viable. A case in point is Facebook, whose active users make up over a quarter of the globe's population. Android and Apple users can also choose from well over two million apps, yet Apple's App Store began with just 500 applications from third-party developers. So, just as with social networking or mobile software marketplaces, a tech start-up might begin with a strategy of creating a new form of value. These were in a sense dogs at one stage – with low market growth and share – but they grew and grew, developing market share in a market they created themselves. Here, unlike in a conventional market, it was the right move to invest in the dog.

Lots of tech start-ups will be in the low market share/high market growth wildcat section of the matrix. They might have a breakthrough innovation to offer in an existing space, or be attracting receptive customers. But opinions will probably differ on how long their product will be desirable, and so how far the investment should be supported. Such wildcat product initiatives may get into profit and grow fast, but they still suggest high uncertainty and risk. Their funding needs might be very high, but if they make it, the payoffs could be high too. Only investors with a taste for risk will go for these kinds of start-up ventures.

Stars are product concepts which already have a high share of a high-growth market. They may need further funding, in order to keep growing fast in such a competitive market. Stars in the tech world will also make for high value creation for investors, even if the company isn't making profits. Stars won't be looking for early capital injection, or even be in the early rounds of financing. Rather than helping kick-start, investors will want to give large amounts of funding for **scaling up**. For them, the risk is lower because the concept is pretty much proven. The share ownership investors can get at this stage will be much lower than for investors who took the big risks earlier on. Arguably, star status should be the end game for a tech start-up – rather than aiming to become a cash cow like a traditional business. This is because start-ups need to keep innovating, driving market expansion and growing their own share in that market. Low market growth, regardless of share, probably wouldn't be something a tech start-up would aim for. So, the growth share matrix suggests that a tech start-up could be a dog or a wildcat at the outset, but aim to become a star, achieving great success, though requiring continuous steering. As such, the growth share matrix gives us a really useful guide to what tech start-ups should pursue, which goes against the grain of conventional corporate strategy. It can guide us towards entrepreneurial pathways where we have to keep a close eye on market share and growth, with a view to attaining stardom rather than cowdom!

The next step would be to look at the life cycle of a product. Figure 2.2 shows us what the growth phase would be like for a conventional product, where sales are going up and the market is expanding. After launch, if a product's market grows, it will face increased competition, with some weaker businesses dropping out of the market, until a maturity plateau is reached. Then, just a few major players stick around, each with high market share. When demand for the product starts to drop off, it will start to go into decline.

For traditional industrial products, the growth share matrix tells us that if a wildcat gets funded, and gains market share, it will become a star. After some intense competition, only a few stars will

**Figure 2.2** The life cycle of a product

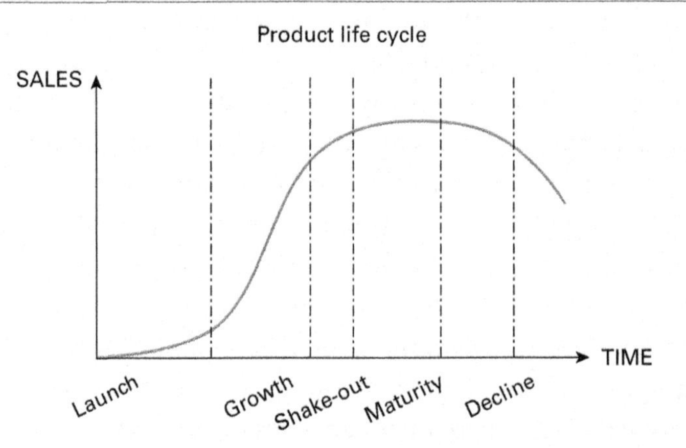


emerge, with some finally becoming cash cows. When the product reaches the end of its maturity phase, an alternative innovation will replace it. Once both market growth and share are in decline, the product will fall into the dog category, and faces being deleted altogether. Figure 2.3 shows a product's path from one cycle to the next.

**Figure 2.3** Traditional product transition across the growth share matrix

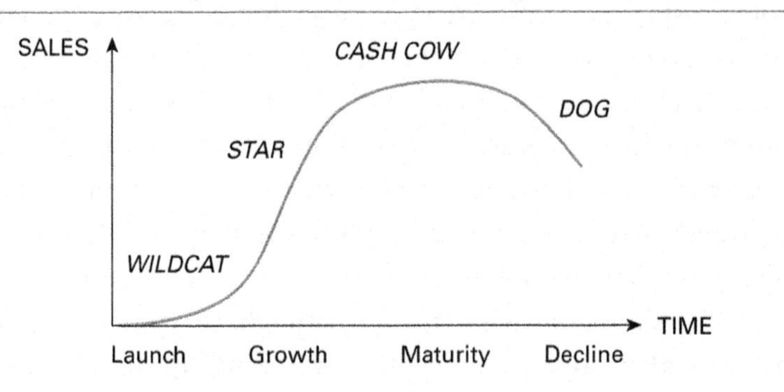


Tech products follow a different growth path. As we've seen, a dog or wildcat tech start-up might go for funding in the hope of becoming a star. But ideally, a tech product wouldn't then become a cash cow, because high market share should trigger further market growth. So, *a successful tech start-up needs to stay in the star matrix quadrant* – enjoying high market share but at the same time creating further growth for the market it inhabits. Figure 2.4 shows this revised product life cycle path. The dog or wildcat start-up that launches successfully might produce profit or create value. Either one of these means it becomes a star. Then, it might upgrade its product and launch an updated version, so the start-up keeps its star status. Its market share will grow, at the same time as the market itself grows, supporting further market share. Profits will go up with each launch of a new product version. If there are profits that translate into cash flows, the start-up can use these to finance some of its business activities. But more likely, the value they create will draw more investment funding, and the start-up can scale up the business.

**Figure 2.4** Tech product transition across the growth share matrix

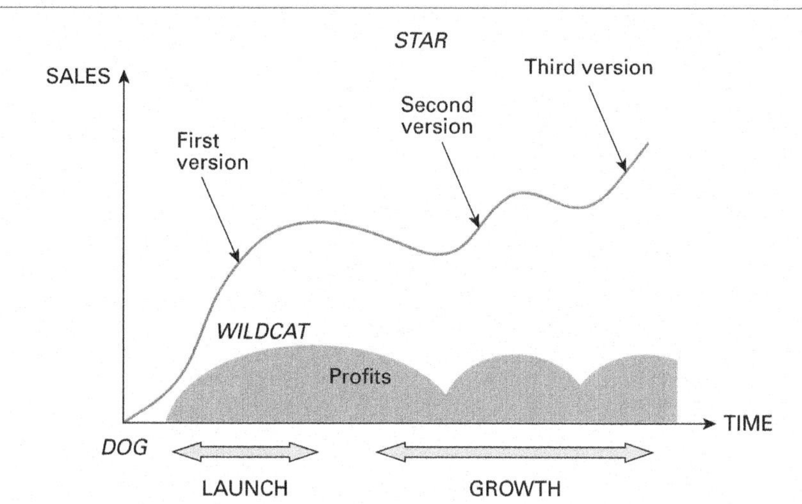


## Let's be strategic

Let's take a look at Michael Porter's 'five forces' model. Porter (1979, 1980, 1985, 2001) is seen by many as the godfather of corporate strategy. His model helped a whole generation of business people think about how competitive forces in their industries affect corporate profits. The five forces include:

- ✔ the number and capabilities of your competitors;
- ✔ the ability of your customers to find a substitute for your product;
- ✔ the potential threat posed by competitors;

- ✔ the ease with which your suppliers can raise prices;
- ✔ the ease with which your customers could get you to lower your prices.

Porter also came up with three generic strategies for firms making abnormally high profits. Some companies seek **cost leadership** by cutting their costs so they can offer lower prices to their customers. Some use a **differentiation** approach and gain market share with a unique product that customers really value and will pay a premium for. And then, some adopt a **focus** strategy, using either of the above approaches but in a niche market that competitors can't service. A company that doesn't do well with either cost leadership or differentiation will at best achieve average profits, but probably won't even be viable. Figure 2.5 shows the possibilities.

**Figure 2.5** Cost leadership vs differentiation matrix

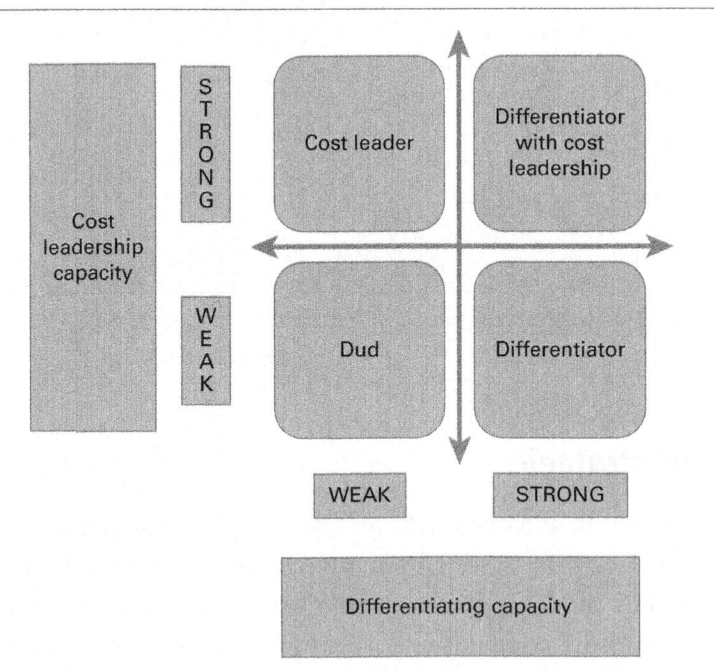


Porter's view is that these five forces need to be balanced in your favour to give your company the most power. You can then adopt either a cost leadership or differentiation strategy, and you will come out on top. But as a tech start-up, you would do better by seeking to unbound limits, creating value through interconnections and by integrating aspects of single value chains. A tech start-up shouldn't be trying to limit how much competitors or customers can reduce their commercial potential, as the five forces suggest. Instead, it can look for different ways to create value. E-tailers such as Amazon, for example, give customers the option of buying from third-party sellers (and Amazon gets commissions and knowledge of commercial activity from these sales). Tech firms can re-distribute value by disrupting business models. They can give back some value to customers through cheaper pricing, but also keep some of that value created in-house.

Take, for instance, Airbnb's impact on travel accommodation. As mentioned in Chapter 1, this is a tech leader in the 'sharing economy', enabling private property owners to let out any spare capacity. It's made it very easy for suppliers to enter the market, and for travellers to search for them. Their technology has also pushed the transactions costs right down, so Airbnb's cut can be very low but with volume driving profits. Airbnb hasn't tried to compete with hotels, which would have meant investing in real estate, room provision, service systems and all the traditional patron services. Instead, it has looked to an alternative source of existing capacity, and that way it has drawn in both new providers and traditional ones. The flexibility Airbnb gives suppliers is also extreme and novel: people offering accommodation can add or remove listings whenever they want. Airbnb has pushed down hotel revenues by 10 per cent in many global cities, and the value this creates, for customers and for itself, keeps rising as listings grow. This means hotels are left with the same cost bases as before, but lower business to cover those costs. Their profits go down, so their value does too. The value Airbnb has created comes from the savings consumers make on costs, and this is redistributed away from hotels, going back to customers and to Airbnb itself. The company also creates market growth, as travellers tend to start using accommodation more often, rather than just substituting one kind of accommodation for another. Naturally, Airbnb has serious costs around its technological platform, with a business model that is set for value growth. It's the top name in this new, tech-based commercial space, so it wields a lot of market power. Investors have valued Airbnb three times higher than the second largest global hotel group (Johnson, 2017).

Uber's impact is very similar to that of Airbnb. Their technology makes for flexibility, and value gets distributed away from traditional taxi and minicab firms. Instead it goes to drivers using their own vehicles, with Uber's technological support, who offer alternative travel options to customers. A technology-enabled platform like Uber 'provides many advantages and lower prices for consumers compared with the traditional taxi cab dispatch system, and this has boosted demand for ride services, which, in turn, has increased total demand for workers with the requisite skills to work as for-hire drivers, potentially raising earnings for all workers with such skills' (Hall, 2015). Not everyone sees only advantages. Some worry about the costs of having a new army of independent workers in the sharing economy (Goudin, 2016; Hancock, 2014). Others are concerned that the full benefits of the sharing economy won't spread across large economic regions (Journalist's Resource, 2017). But what is absolutely clear is that, for start-ups, technology is the key to disrupting traditional business models. This isn't just because of new capabilities, but because these technologies can be made available and used so widely. While the tech firm invests in developing the web platform to enable peer-to-peer transactions, customers and suppliers themselves invest in the technology too, using it on their own devices. So even though the business model relies on technology, the start-up doesn't take on the total expenses required to have it. This is in sharp contrast with traditional businesses, which would usually have to absorb all the costs of a corporate offering. In terms of Porter's forces, suppliers and customers facilitate cost savings for a tech company, given their ownership of the technology. When profits start coming in the returns can then be very high, as we'll see in Chapter 5.

Ola, Didi Chixing and Uber are fairly large platforms whereas Grabonrent, Seekmi and Rent-a-Suitcase are emerging in the sharing economy. How does trust get established? They have the advantage of user rating systems, which inspire trust in customers. Traditional firms in many sectors, including hotels, have had to invest in branding and training to achieve the same effect. Airbnb and Travelmob create further value by allowing suppliers to work flexibly, in terms of working hours and when to provide the service. The market ecosystem that their technology produces gets rid of many costs that more traditional market players would incur. So, in Figure 2.5, a tech start-up doesn't just succeed because it offers an innovation that is different from traditional products or services. Its success is also partly through cost leadership – because of the way its customers and suppliers use its technology. That is, it resides in the top right-hand quadrant. In the industrial economy, this wouldn't be plausible. This is because high-volume production and mass marketing are associated with cost leadership for abnormal profit generation. If a company went for differentiation, charging premium prices for a customized product, it would be looking at a much smaller customer base. For a tech start-up, mass customization, along with both innovation and differentiation, creates new possibilities. It can be *both a cost leader and a differentiator.*

## *Always aim for high profit/high volume?*

We've seen that the growth share matrix and Porter's model both need a serious makeover if they're going to be useful in today's tech start-up environment. In their original form, their value for us now lies in showing us what not to do. But what about customer volume and profitability? It's just common sense that if you make a larger, rather than a smaller, profit on every product you sell, and you sell more of these products, your overall profits will grow. So, any business should make sure their products contribute as much as possible to profit, and make the highest sales they can. In Figure 2.6, it's the top right quadrant, A, you want to be in – with a high volume of sales, as well as high contribution from each sale. B products are profitable at the unit level, but you need to sell more of them to get higher profits. C products give low profit per unit, or even make a loss, so could be the most problematic. They need to move up the profit contribution line. D products might also be making a loss, but are only selling in low numbers.

For tech start-ups, there are a few questions we need to ask. First, we should look at the people who are actually using a firm's output. Are they paying directly for this, or are the paying customers coming to you because they're attracted by these consumers? People using Google to search online don't have to pay: it's the advertisers who are Google's customers, and generate revenue for the company. It's the same for Newsmax. They have users who consume what the platform enables, but the actual customers are the advertisers and companies that purchase user data. To a certain extent, then, *the user is the product*, since users represent eyeballs that advertisers pay for. Google wants users to make a high volume of searches, with the product costing Google quite a bit before it can be delivered to the customer (the advertisers). Newsmax likewise has the task of delivering the right kinds of users to ads, and the right data to paying customers. If users are the product, then Google and Newsmax have quadrant C as their objective for them, rather than A. This despite the fact that, like all commercial businesses, they ultimately want a large base of customers who buy products, and to get high profits on these.

**Figure 2.6** Unit profit vs consumer volume

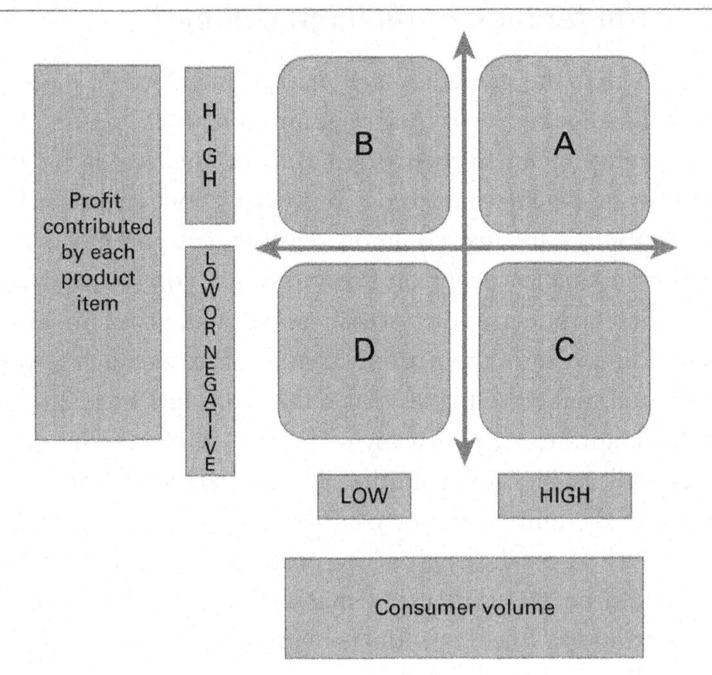


What this really means is that, for them, there isn't a direct link between the resources they use and the source of revenue. Similarly, their costs don't link directly to their sales. Tech start-ups can disrupt traditional value-creation models so much that new lines get drawn, and these make consumers distinct from customers. If your service users are the product, and your customers paying for the product don't get a say in the form of that product, your financial management is going to be different. It'll need to be founded on a very different premise from traditional companies. We'll look at the metrics in a later chapter on this. What's clear is that the volume of users matters immensely. The profit-per-customer only has a very indirect relationship with consumer volume.

A second point that affects some start-ups is that connections between products matter. If, as we saw with Google, the people consuming your output are your product, then you need to grow that product base. There are real opportunities to do this if products get value out of interconnections. We refer to this as the company having **network effects**. So, users of TripAdvisor, for instance, get greater value out of it as the base of TripAdvisor users grows. Once there is some content, it attracts consumers of that content, and they start to contribute to the content themselves. This then attracts more users. So, *consumers become producers of content, which fuels further user engagement*. The greater the value to each user, the more the network grows in size. Any tech start-up with similar network effects should grow its user base quickly, since that growth carries with it implicit value. Google's searches likewise grow in quality as more users carry out searches, because information from past searches is fed back into the algorithms, enhancing future output. Alibaba also naturally attracts users (buyers) if it has more users (sellers), and sellers are also attracted as the number of buyers goes up. Indeed.com attracts job-seekers because of the number of job advertisers, and that number goes up as the volume of job-seekers grows. As with our earlier point, user numbers matter a great deal because the more users there are, the more will flock to the service provider.

When all market competitors in the same space understand the power of networks, the competition to '*get big fast*' becomes intense very rapidly. A platform with lots of users but only a small base of customers won't generate revenues, let alone make profits. To attract customers, it's essential to have more users. If your existing users promote more user growth, as with TripAdvisor, then this becomes the vehicle for larger-scale growth. You'll attract more customers who eventually drive the company's growth, value creation and profitability. The Catch 22 here is that lack of customers means less funds for promotion and technical refinement aimed at user growth, and these can be expensive. But without high user growth, customers won't be attracted to the company anyway. You need high user growth to drive high customer growth, which then leads back to more user growth.

In the same way that the spiral can be downward if the start-up can't attract both users and customers rapidly enough, it can also be positive. Once a threshold is reached, user growth can drive customer growth fast, and vice versa. Kick-starting a positive spiral is vital for tech start-ups that can show network effects. It's the kick-starting that is difficult to do without funding. Yet, as we'll see in Chapter 7, investors sometimes only look for very high-growth-potential start-ups, with a chance at fast-paced growth. And this is something that a firm can achieve via network effects.

We've said that getting to a threshold volume of a product's users can trigger more volume growth, and when the scale of that volume picks up, it can generate extreme value growth. It's worth noting that, when a company provides a service to users, this increases the costs on a one-to-one basis. That's to say, the company incurs costs at the same rate as the number of users grows. But, past a certain point where users get value out of other users joining the platform, value just grows at an accelerating rate. As we'll explain below, we need to think through the costing mechanics carefully if we want to get to that threshold volume point. The secret lies in understanding that *costs grow linearly, but value expands exponentially*!

A third feature tech start-ups should think about is that people like familiarity. Technology which gives a sense of comfort by using particular standards, modes of interface, or ease of manoeuvrability, tends to make users more resistant to change. Look at Blackberry's decline over the past decade, from having one in five smartphone users globally using its device to only one in a thousand today. In the end, the company abandoned making phones altogether. Yet many users still lament the decline of Blackberry, listing its advantages such as its physical keyboard, lack of distractions from games, lightning-fast e-mail and slick operating system. Standards, once established, keep customers coming back. They are loyal because there is system stickiness. Changing a web-based e-mail is likewise costly as it means users have to learn a new approach and update all their contacts. Users of Microsoft Windows face **lock-in** to a high degree, as they'll then buy into a whole ecosystem of applications. Switching to another platform becomes a hard decision. But companies do sometimes start new standards to displace other market players. Apple killed off floppy drives, CD-ROM drives and smartphone physical keyboards. Its recent iPhone has done away with headphone jacks, forcing customers to opt for an adapter or, hopefully, move to wireless headphones. Market leaders can effect change. Market followers follow. *Tech standards that become established help companies maintain and develop market share.* So, tech start-ups need to either add capability and complement an industry leader's offering, or come up with new innovations which create new domains of value.

So, if we use a growth share matrix perspective to think about tech start-ups, we'd suggest that investing in a dog company is the best start. This dog would have to gain enough *traction* to generate market need. This would create market share growth, which in turn triggers more demand. This would then mobilize further market growth. We've seen that network effects and lock-ins are mechanisms through which this can happen. Once market growth is kick-started, the dog moves into a wildcat position, or might go straight into star status with high share and high market growth. Maybe the tech start-up is in a market that is being established, and already has competing companies. In this case, the wildcat firm might try to get ahead through differentiation, and become a star. It could gain market share in a growing market, and one which it tries to redefine to mirror its focused advantage. This is pretty much what Facebook did when it challenged MySpace, which had been the market leader up until 2008. MySpace had what effectively became Facebook's future audience. Its technological infrastructure was sound, and it got positive reviews from users and the press. After News Corporation acquired MySpace in 2005, it was armed with the technological back-up it needed to become the main social media giant. Indeed, we could say that MySpace started social networking as a dog.

But Facebook overtook MySpace to become the social media juggernaut it now is (Schenker, 2015). Likewise, Google overshadowed search engines such as Yahoo, Ask Jeeves and AltaVista, despite being late to the party. Google was the wildcat which fast gained market share in a growing market, displacing the others. Today, we could call both Google and Facebook stars. They continuously create and grow markets, and develop 'needs' by providing solutions. It is the wise thing to do for a tech start-up to go for star status and stay there, rather than trying to move into a cash cow position. Slowing market growth is unlikely to be a good space for tech businesses. But stars, while they may make cash, will probably need ongoing investment, infrastructural back-up and monitoring. Companies like Spotify, Farfetch, Snapdeal and Airbnb are stars which do not rest. They have to continuously create the product and the market, expanding and reforming them. To stay ahead, you have to keep creating novel concepts which generate and define more emerging needs. Unlike in the industrial context, cashing in on cows is not the best goal for a tech start-up.

We've also seen that Porter's framing of the issues can tell us how different things are today. Past strategies can be countered with new technologies which allow us to re-distribute and/or create value. Rather than using a pure 'five forces' focus, tech firms have altered the dynamics of competition. They can completely bypass the hurdles that are there for the industrial economy. This means we need to think again about the best business strategies for tech firms, and how they can become start-up leaders. A tech start-up can combine mass customization, innovation and differentiation, so it becomes a cost leader as well as a differentiator. This leads us to the question of whether high market volume must co-exist with high profits from sales. Further, we've seen that, for a tech start-up, thinking through the difference between customers and consumers is really important. *Customers generate revenues, and consumers generate costs*. This breaks the links between the two in a way that hasn't been part of conventional industrial business. It means we need to think differently about profit-per-sale and consumer growth. On top of that, many tech firms enjoy network effects. Because value can grow exponentially, while costs show only linear growth, this puts a totally different spin on how we manage resources and grow our firm, rather than trying to maximize profits immediately.

Additionally, technology can help you to ring-fence your customers within an ecosystem, and alter your product standards to crowd out competitors. Taken together, these effects mean growth in user volume and value creation are particularly significant for tech start-ups. We'll look into this more in the chapters that follow.

## Risk and potential

Anyone can have a good idea. Those who can make them happen change the world. But changing the world requires money, and how to release and manage finance is at the heart of this book. We'll see over and over again that technology isn't all there is to making money from technology. Key to a start-up's success is its ability to commercially operationalize an idea founded on a technological precept. A start-up has to show that an idea is viable and feasible. Much of this comes from evidence that a market already exists around the product concept, and that it can grow. But we also need to see that the team leading the start-up has the wherewithal to carry the start-up to success. And finally, that once resources are in place, the start-up will attain pre-set **milestones** which, if missed, could lead to the start-up's 'death in the valley'. Riskiness is inherent to tech start-ups. What types of risks exist?

Start-ups face two broad categories of risks. The first is the **business risk** around the product, the technology or the market. For instance, there could be issues with the product if its quality, features or delivery preferences aren't up to scratch. There might be technological failings when it comes to development, provision or servicing of the product. Perhaps your intended customers aren't receptive to the product concept. The market could be too small, or shifting too fast towards other solutions. These are all potential business risks. We've seen above the elements of technology which affect business risk. The other category relates to the **financial risk** of the start-up. How the business funds itself, and the form of its cost structure, will affect the risks a start-up faces. Over the past decade, both types of risks have altered across pretty much all business markets, industries and platforms – new and old. As a result, opportunities for tech start-ups to create value have expanded very quickly, but so have the challenges and risks.

Assessing risk is a conditioned reflex for most people. Deciding on a course of action usually involves looking at the value of the desired outcome, and weighing this against the costs of acting, as well as looking for possible unintended effects. We usually make financial decisions with a view that the rewards should take account of the risks we absorb. A sure thing carries little risk, so the payoff should be smaller than those we'd expect from a risky proposition, where there's a chance of low returns or even losses. It's important to consider the timing of expected payoffs, too. A remote payoff means a longer wait for the returns, and higher risks that they never show. In investment thinking, it's usually accepted that risk–return relationships should show balance. An investor who founds a business that has potential for high returns will do so in the knowledge that there's a high degree of risk. If they underestimate risks, their profits will take a hit. So, **due diligence** is essential. This means that investors will look at how viable a concept is at the outset, and how well the start-up can sustain successful operations in the longer run.

Investors will assess a tech start-up's idea, the market and the team in particular, to be confident that they can deliver. In terms of the *product concept* and *market*, an investor will look for a competitive differentiating feature. Perhaps the start-up can better execute something that already has an existing market. Or it might offer an entirely new business model or market to be developed. Perhaps the product has lock-in capability where, as we saw earlier, there is resistance for a customer to move away once they've adopted a product in terms of effort and time. If the concept enjoys network effects, this could be a very attractive opportunity, where fast business development and growth become important. The investor will also want to see whether there is uniqueness in the technology, and how far the concept has been developed by the time they step in. As part of investor due diligence, they will look at who the entrepreneurs are. The *team* needs to have both solid technical expertise and sales orientation. It also needs to be comfortable with acting on advice, and be flexible around investors' executive approach and decision-making. This could include times when the investors signal a need to pivot the business along a new trajectory. Investors won't want a team to show emotional resistance to evolving their product concept or business hypothesis. A founder who only wants to stay with the start-up short-term, or wants to stay in a specific role long-term, won't impress an investor.

Tech start-ups tend to have a low chance of high payoffs in the long term, but a high chance of large immediate cash needs! But this isn't a problem – in fact it's what makes them attractive to investors. If the payoffs are likely to be positive but not very high, this wouldn't excite tech investors. And if a start-up's funding needs are low where there are high expected returns, it's likely the funding will have been met through other means. If an investor likes there to be high variability of returns, that means they are not **risk-averse**. Looking purely at the risk–return dimension of an investment, such an investor will seek high-risk/high-return characteristics, which are generally what a tech start-up has. We look at different sources of funding in Chapters 6 and 7 and see that different investors will have different aims. In terms of market opportunity, some venture capital investors may only look for start-ups that show evidence of a clear market opportunity with possible future sales (possibly of the order of $300 million within five years where 20–25 per cent of the market could be captured). Earlier investors may want a larger share of ownership and show different risk–return preferences. *Pegging risk to the level of expected returns is what always underpins investment decisions.* Of course, there's no point in an investor taking high risks for a low level of expected payoffs, or for only a tiny portion of a high expected value. So, the investor who takes the risk will ask for as big a share of the company as possible. We'll see later in the book how to avoid giving up too much control or ownership. But for now, the point is that tech start-ups have a special kind of financial risk, aside from the business risk issues we looked at earlier.

Tech firms by definition invest and deal in technology. Initially there may be low entry costs to get into a market and the capital required may be small at the outset. But with some scaling up as the start-up gets market traction, bigger investments at a high price will have to be made to expand. Technologies change fast and can quickly become obsolete. Customer loyalties may change, especially in the face of new disruptive technologies. So, *most investment costs don't tend to retain value once they've been incurred*. Code can also be expensive to create, but may have little value after it is developed. Unlike buildings and land, tech firms invest in costs that are of little use to others, and these costs tend to be high. But by the same token, because tech firms' products tend to lack physical attributes, the production costs don't go up with the volume of sales. There may be some back-up service to each sale, but these can often be provided online and at minimal cost. So, if your business has high investment needs, but low operational costs once you've developed your product, then what you need is a good customer base. Once you've covered your initial costs from these customer purchases, most of what you then sell translates into profits.

This could be what is beautiful about your tech start-up. But it could also be its bane. This is because the allure of such high profits leads many players into the marketplace. And after a while, we'll find that there's *only room for a few players*. Everyone wants the lion's share of such a high-value business. So, everyone will initially sacrifice on profit to build market share and they'll watch other emerging differentiated features introduced by competitors and try to counter these with further development of the product or platform. After a while, the last firm standing makes all the money. *Winner takes all* in technology markets – sometimes this is short lived but in its two-decade history, the internet economy has shown many instances of this.

Investors into tech start-ups are aware of this and will do their due diligence to be sure that the start-up they back will be the last one standing. But the uncertainty will remain high and they may end up sinking a lot of resources into your business, only to see it fail. Their ownership share will reflect the risk they're willing to take. The risk profile of tech firms tells us there's only room for a few players because of the structure of costs. This means possible high returns to investors but definite high risks. So the types of costs you incur in your tech start-up will affect the risk concerns of your investors. Increasingly, because of different technology options you can use, you'll have alternatives to choose from regarding the types of costs you set your business up for and so you can influence the risks your business entails. We'll look at this in detail in Chapter 3.

In addition to cost-structure issues, some tech firms might enjoy network effects. As discussed above, once their user volume reaches a certain threshold point it starts to snowball, and more users want the service. This just intensifies the reality that there's only room for a few players. Technology solutions of this kind tend, by their very nature, to dominate industries and crowd out other competitors. Just as social media platforms like Facebook generate more user interest the higher the user sign-up rate, the same goes for pure online matchmaking services like Parship where more users imply more potential dates, or Lazada which brings suppliers and buyers together, or Google which gives more refined results the more searches are made. The end result is a market where *there's only room for a very few major incumbents.*

But remember that this can work in reverse too. A platform which is on a growth path because of network effects can be knocked out very quickly too for the same reason. Consider Friendster which was started in 2002 and rapidly attained over a million members. For a while it was the top online social network site. But within two years, MySpace overtook Friendster in terms of page views. MySpace itself gained immense traction but then lost out to Facebook five years later. So network effects can catapult a company's growth but also work in reverse – as rapidly. Investors take account of the risks where network potential can sponsor fast growth but equally take away value when users flock to another alternative which also enjoys network effects.

Further, some tech firms aim to operate in environments where there's a lot of slack, or unused capacity, that can be put to use if the right technical infrastructure is in place. Once they've done this, a sharing economy innovation starts to grow, by making the traditional players less attractive. Think of Uber, Lyft, Didi Kuaidi and Ola displacing taxis and other forms of private transport. But usually with such business models, the value taken away from traditional competitors, and that created by new users, reduces profits to a level where only a few providers can exist. In effect, most tech sectors have a few big players and a lot of smaller players. Tech investors are interested in ones which, while risky, show potential to be big, and these are the ones that get funded faster.

Tech start-ups need to adopt strategies and financial management practices which are quite different from traditional economy businesses, in terms of homing in on the right strategic options and making correct risk–return assessments. In the next chapters, we'll take a tour of the underlying financial structures that you need to understand to successfully finance and manage your tech start-up.

## Summary of chapter

We've reviewed why tech start-ups:

- must manage continuous feedback loops of information;
- should use conventional strategic thinking in a contrarian way;
- differ across costs, volume and value-creation dimensions;
- have risk–return characteristics which affect how finance is raised and managed.

## Review questions

1. Why do tech start-ups operate within continuous feedback loops?
2. What is an example of a tech start-up that is a 'dog' in the growth share matrix?
3. Why is a 'star' the end game for tech start-ups?
4. Why do some platforms have revenues generated by their customers and costs produced by their users?
5. What types of risks do tech start-ups present to investors?

## Further reading

Martinez, AG (2016) *Chaos Monkeys: Obscene fortune and random failure in Silicon Valley*, Harper, New York

Thiel, P and Masters, B (2014) *Zero to One: Notes on start-ups, or how to build the future*, Penguin Random House, New York

## References

Goudin, P (2016) The cost of non-Europe in the sharing economy: Economic, social and legal challenges and opportunities (European Parliamentary Research Service paper PE 558.777), available from http://www.europarl.europa.eu/RegData/etudes/STUD/2016/558777/EPRS_STU(2016)558777_EN.pdf [accessed 21.3.17]

Hall, J (2015) An analysis of the labor market for Uber's driver partners in the United States, available from s3.amazonaws.com/uber-static/comms/PDF/Uber_Driver-Partners_Hall_Kreuger_2015.pdf [accessed 21.3.17]

Hancock, M (2014) Move to make UK global centre for sharing economy (DBIS Press Release), available from www.gov.uk/government/news/move-to-make-uk-global-centre-for-sharing-economy [accessed 21.3.17]

Henderson, B (1970) The product portfolio, available from www.bcgperspectives.com/content/classics/strategy_the_product_portfolio/ [accessed 21.3.17]

Johnson, M (2017) Will Airbnb be the next tech unicorn to IPO in 2017?, available from www.zacks.com/stock/news/262357/will-airbnb-be-the-next-tech-unicorn-to-ipo-in-2017 [accessed 14.6.17]

Journalist's Resource (2017) Uber, Airbnb and consequences of the sharing economy: Research roundup, available from journalistsresource.org/studies/economics/business/airbnb-lyft-uber-bike-share-sharing-economy-research-roundup [accessed 21.3.17]

Porter, ME (1979) How competitive forces shape strategy, *Harvard Business Review*, 57, 2, pp 137–45

Porter, ME (1980) *Competitive Strategy*, Free Press, New York

Porter, ME (1985) *Competitive Advantage*, Free Press, New York

Porter, ME (2001) Strategy and the Internet, *Harvard Business Review*, 79, 3, pp 62–78

Ries, E (2011) *The Lean Start-up: How today's entrepreneurs use continuous innovation to create radically successful businesses*, Crown Business, New York

Schenker, M (2015) Former MySpace CEO explains why MySpace lost out to Facebook so badly, available from www.digitaltrends.com/social-media/former-myspace-ceo-reveals-what-facebook-did-right-to-dominate-social-media/#ixzz4byomXDxi [accessed 21.3.17]

# Start-up contribution analysis

03

Accounting helps conventional businesses to say something about their past performance, as well as to plan their future activities. They can track their actual progress against plans and compare how they are doing relative to competitors. They'll also be able to use accounting to manage cash and decide on how much funding they require and of course, to communicate to investors and others about their activities. Typically, industrial enterprises use accounting information to:

- access finance;
- monitor their performance;
- assess their financial state of play when needed;
- report to investors and other parties on their activities.

Tech start-ups also need information for all these activities. But for them, life is more complex. It's hard for start-ups to get information about other similar businesses that share objectives with them. This means there aren't so many external benchmarks, which they could use to guide their own activities, or to communicate with investors or lenders. This extreme lack of business and market information and the uncertainty tech start-ups face means it's essential for them to experiment with and explore growth possibilities. In this chapter, we'll look at the building blocks of how accounting can assist. We'll learn:

- about the start-up financial control loop;
- how we work out financial contribution and track its impact on the start-up;
- why it's crucial to know what your variable and fixed costs are;
- how to achieve break-even;
- ways to use financial intelligence to guide operational and strategic actions.

## The start-up financial control loop

Start-ups need to keep tweaking their activities on the basis of any new information they get, altering their business model as they go. A start-up still needs to have a formal process for this exploratory way of operating, that will help it in:

- ✔ planning its activities;
- ✔ acting on desired pursuits;
- ✔ monitoring outcomes;
- ✔ changing and refining any new action plans;
- ✔ keeping investors informed and reassured.

To be successful, the start-up needs to have a mechanism for internalizing any new information it gets from the external business world, and from its own operations, to ensure it makes the right changes. Ultimately, a tech start-up must not only be willing to change its business model as it goes, but should actively seek out ways to do this. In other words, pursuing self-change is vital for a tech start-up's viability and growth.

How does a tech start-up manage to do this? It would be great if a start-up could base all its plan on a neat set of anticipated costs and performance targets, drawn from its own experience or that of other companies. This would make it pretty straightforward for the start-up to control and assess all its ongoing activities, and make solid plans. But, tech start-ups don't have the luxury of precedents, or benchmarks, to tell them whether they are on-track. They must first search out information from the market and other sources, and then continuously assess the impact of their own activities. In this chapter, we'll look at the financial control loop, which start-ups can use to bring their financial information into focus. This tool will help tech start-ups to formalize exactly what they need to do when it comes to raising finance in the first place. It then supports start-ups as they engage in a feedback process of planning, acting and monitoring impact, and finally ploughing all this learning back into operations in real time.

Whatever the business may be, a firm's managers must do two basic things: identify what they would like to do; and put those ideas into action. Once you reach a point where you can look at the impact of those actions, you should aim to both measure and explain any deviations from what you expected. On the basis of what you learn, you make new plans to guide future action. This applies to all entrepreneurs. Your business pursuits should be founded on a hypothesis, which you see as supporting the business model you choose. However, you should *always be looking to learn from your actions along the way*, including why your aims did not pan out as expected, and to what degree. Figure 3.1 shows what the *tech start-up financial control loop* looks like.

**Figure 3.1** The tech start-up financial control loop

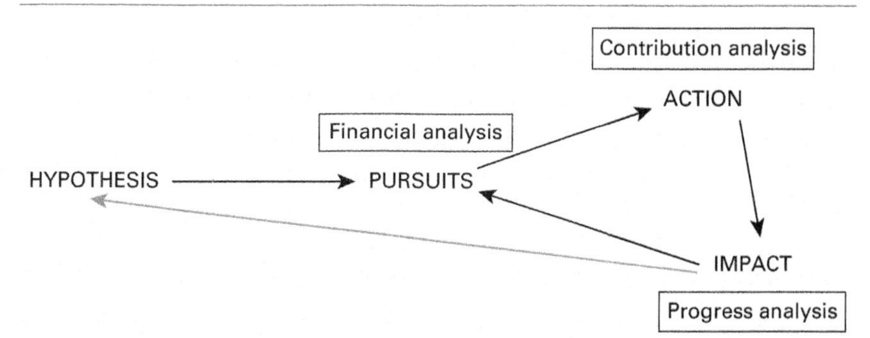


We will see that there are three essential steps for the financial control of a tech start-up. This chapter looks at the first step. It covers what we need to know about costs, so we can work out how actions link to what a start-up can yield financially (*contribution analysis*). We also need to get a handle on the accounting statements which allow us to undertake a *financial analysis* of the business pursuits, and which we cover in Chapter 4. Finally, in Chapter 5 we'll consider the third step, which is to assess financial impact metrics (*progress analysis*). Doing this can tell us something about the impact of your start-up's activities, and how we can use this information to monitor and rethink the business hypothesis if required. This will also assist when looking at options for sourcing finance.

## Financial control in three steps

So, it's clear that tech start-ups really are different from industrial-age organizations. Because of this, they need a specific financial outlook. If we can get to grips with the different accounting basis that tech businesses need, we'll be able to better manage their activities. This will help us to harness their potential for profit and value maximization.

In this chapter, we'll go through the first of the three main steps towards understanding the financial plumbing of a tech enterprise. The three steps are:

*Step 1*: Look at the cost changes a start-up goes through as it becomes active, and assess these in accounting terms (this chapter).

*Step 2*: Figure out how to communicate business performance in financial terms, so we can steer the enterprise towards the entrepreneur's vision (Chapter 4).

*Step 3*: Get a handle on financial monitoring, so we can control operations through a feedback loop of information and identify how to raise finance (Chapter 5).

So, let's get started with Step 1.

**Profit**, in economic terms, is simply the difference between revenues (or sales) and costs. Naturally, to understand our profits, we need to be able to measure both our revenues and our costs. Unlike traditional firms, for lots of tech businesses, the sources of their revenues and costs are different. These kinds of businesses often attract *customers who generate revenues* for them on the one hand, while on the other hand having a base of very different *consumers who give rise to most of the costs*. Let's start by looking at the cost side of tech businesses.

A **cost** is a measure, in monetary terms, of what you give up to acquire a product. Most businesses have lots of different cost categories.

Some obvious costs, like electricity, lighting and heating, we label as **expenses**. When we come to write our financial statement (a 'profit and loss statement', or an 'income statement' discussed in Chapter 4), we represent all our expenses like these alongside our income for that period. For a start-up, there may well be some **expenditures** on things that are going to help generate income at some point. This might be something you buy, such as a 3D printer, which you expect to last for, say, three years. These kinds of costs remain unexpired until they become expenses. An unexpired cost is something that you would typically refer to as an **asset** of your business – such as the 3D printer just purchased. As we'll see in Chapter 4, when creating your balance sheet, as part of your financial statement, these unexpired costs will appear alongside the **liabilities** and **net worth** of the business. But, as you use your 3D printer to make products, and it gradually loses some of its value and future usefulness, what change takes place in accounting terms? Well, over time, your 3D printer is changing from being an asset to being an expense. Put in more technical terms, we need to visualize the behaviour of costs, like the printer, which expire as the firm engages in its operations.

We can simplify how we think about cost behaviour by categorizing patterns into two types: Fixed and Variable. Let's start with **variable costs**. Consider the cost per unit of the products your business might make. For each unit, there might be material costs as production takes place, electricity costs to power a machine, and packaging costs as sales progress. So, if your 3D printer makes product A which takes up, say, £5 of resin per unit printed, then the total direct material cost of manufacturing 10,000 units is £50,000; 20,000 units require direct resin material of £100,000; and so on. The total variable costs go up with increased printing activity (see Figure 3.2). The unit cost of the direct material (£5) remains constant however many units you print (we can ignore for now suppliers offering lower prices at higher volumes which alter the numbers a bit but not the general behaviour of the variable costs). The variable cost per unit does not alter as activity levels change, as shown in Figure 3.3.

Now let's look at fixed costs. A **fixed cost** is one which remains constant in total terms. Consider the 3D printer. Suppose you paid £600,000 for the printer, and assume it has a life of three years. The

**Figure 3.2** Total variable cost behaviour

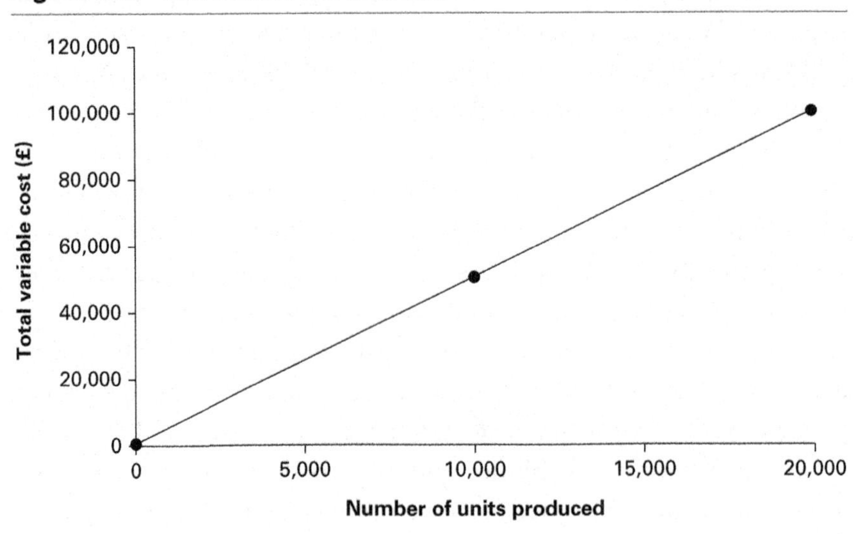

**Figure 3.3** Unit variable cost behaviour

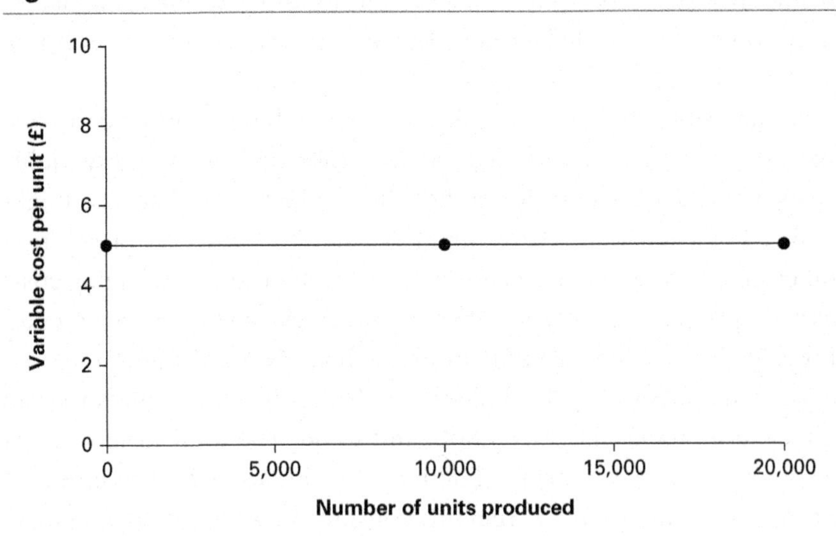


diminution in the cost of the asset every year (or its 'straight-line **depreciation**') would be £200,000. This would not change regardless of whether you used the printer to print 10,000 units or 20,000 units during each year (see Figure 3.4). This means that the 3D printer's cost on a per unit basis decreases as activity levels increase. The reverse is also true: if the volume of activity decreases, the unit cost of the printer effectively increases. So, if we think of the printer's straight-line depreciation in terms of units, we would say: the unit cost of straight-line depreciation of £200,000 for 10,000 units is £20, but for 20,000 units of product, the unit cost is £10 (see Figure 3.5). Other examples of fixed costs, then, would be employees' annual

**Figure 3.4** Total fixed cost behaviour

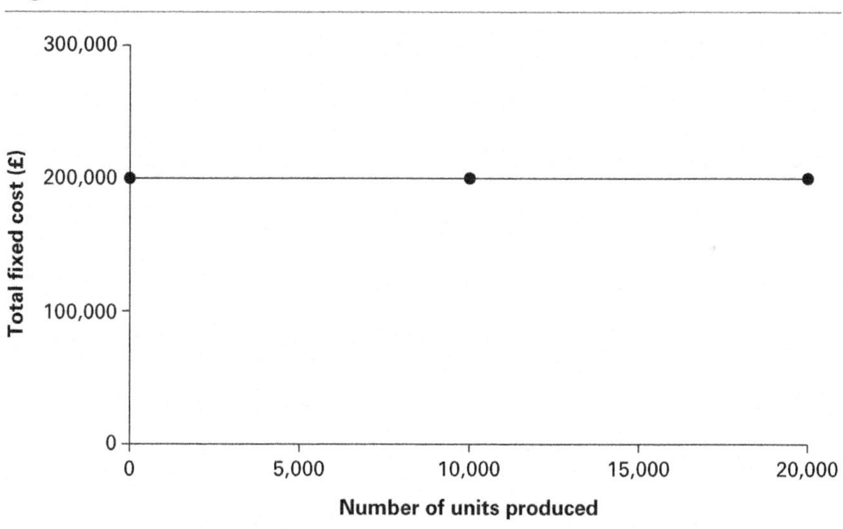


**Figure 3.5** Unit fixed cost behaviour

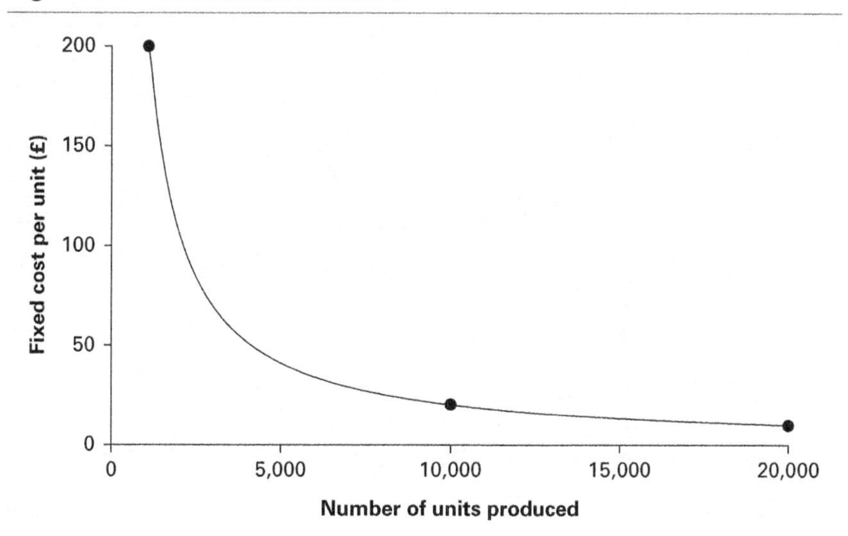

salary or a quarterly insurance bill. They remain the same, however many units are produced in a year. But their unit cost increases if the number of units produced decreases, and vice versa.

So, not all costs vary in relation to activity changes in the same way. Some alter with operational activity and others remain constant. What's significant is that both variable and fixed costs exhibit their particular cost behaviours over defined relevant ranges.

What is a **relevant range**? Let's say that your 3D printer can only print 100 units per hour. This would mean that a second printer will be required if between 101 and 200 units are to be printed every hour. So, the relevant range of the printer is 100 units per hour. Fixed costs are assumed to remain fixed only until the 3D printer reaches its maximum printing capacity. Likewise, the variable cost per unit printed stays the same in spite of activity changes, but only over the relevant volume range of printing. To keep things simple, accountants tend to assume away cost changes per unit that arise from economies of scale, increased productivity or operating efficiencies over the relevant range. Say the supply price of packaging material falls once a certain volume purchase triggers a set discount. We could choose to keep things simple by ignoring this saving from bulk-buying, and instead keep the cost of packaging applied to each unit constant: for example, where we have to purchase more and more 3D printers in order to produce up to 300, or 400, or 500 units per hour. This means we have stepwise cost increases (as in Figure 3.6 – sometimes referred to as semi-fixed costs). If the relevant range for a fixed cost diminishes so that we see a jump in cost at very frequent intervals of production volume changes, then a business may just decide to regard these costs as variable costs (just like in Figure 3.2).

So far, we've looked at fixed and variable costs. However, usually costs are not purely fixed or variable as they combine both forms of cost behaviour. Mixed (or semi-variable) costs have a component that stays constant as activity levels change, and another component that varies proportionately with such changes. So, they may increase, but only in part, with increased activity.

Consider a connected iPad that you might use for your business. The iPad works on a plan where you have to pay for data consumption after you pass a certain volume of data download. These charges

**Figure 3.6** Stepwise cost increases

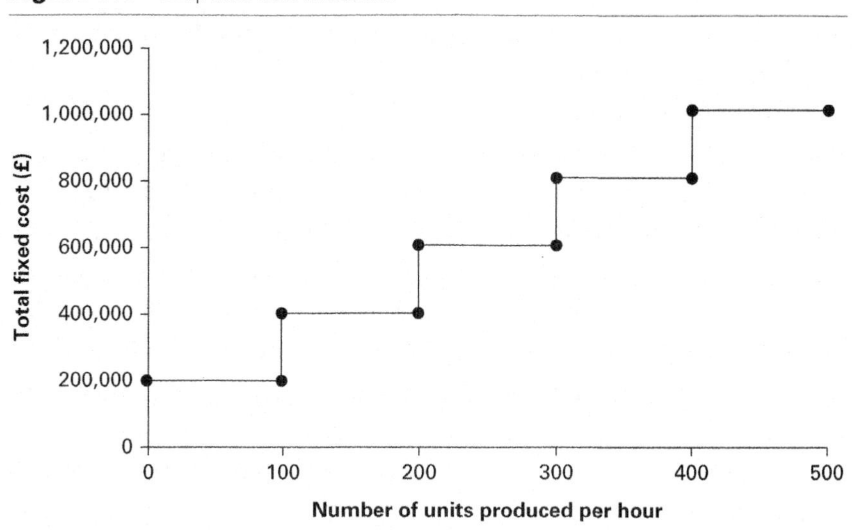


are on top of the standing charge you pay for your connection. This would mean that the total cost of the iPad data usage per period would reflect both a fixed and variable cost component: the standing charge, as well as any extra charges for data over your limit. The same would be true of a salesperson who can earn commission selling iPads on top of their basic salary. The basic salary represents a fixed cost to the retailer, but they also incur a variable cost which depends on the total commission the salesperson makes on iPad sales over a period.

How are costs for a tech business different from costs in other types of businesses? Let's think through the costs involved in more traditional manufacturing such as furniture production. When making physical products, a lot of the raw material used in production, such as the wood used to make tables, might well be directly traceable to the product itself. So, we'd call this a **direct** material cost. There are also some material costs which we could trace to the product, but with only with a huge amount of effort. Imagine each drop of glue used in producing a table. We could monitor these, but it's unlikely to be worth our while. We might find ourselves spending, say, £800 on resources to monitor the usage of glue drops and gain accuracy over a 0.002p cost per drop, for 1,000 tables made. To avoid this, many direct costs that we could theoretically trace to the product, like glue drops, we instead categorize as **indirect**. We can put them into a pool of broad **overhead** costs.

Manufacturing products also involves paying wages to employees. If a business can also trace these directly to the product in a way that is both easy and economical (ie not like counting glue drops), then they can refer to these costs as direct labour costs. Being directly traceable to the product, these direct labour costs rise and fall as production volume rises and falls, making them variable costs like the ones described above. But, businesses often pay an absolute amount – a salary – for labour, ensuring they have the capacity to make their products, regardless of whether or not they fully use that capacity. In that case, it might be better to regard this labour resource as a fixed cost.

Many companies making use of digital technologies have direct labour costs that are a very small fraction of their total costs for making products or providing services. Nowadays, manufacturing companies may well invest in digitization, and so use computer-assisted design, flexible manufacturing systems and industrial robots. This way of working leads to sharply falling levels of not just direct labour input but total labour consumption. Overhead costs represent costs which generally are neither direct labour nor direct material. Over the past century, within manufacturing firms, direct labour as a proportion of total product costs has dropped right down. Instead, we see more and more capital investments in the form of machines and sophisticated production technologies; these enable businesses to create complex products while improving flexibility and to produce customized products in batches of different sizes.

Tech businesses today make even less use of direct labour and very often have no material input whatsoever. Let's look at the production and delivery of Square Enix's *Final Fantasy XV* video game. This requires little material or labour input. The costs are largely fixed costs. It would be theoretically possible to figure out a cost per unit of production, but it would probably be inaccurate in practice, because the fixed costs enable scalability of product provision. Square Enix's cost of sales in 2013 was ¥98.788 billion, and ¥94.794 billion two years later. During that time, its sales went from ¥147.981 billion to ¥167.891 billion. Facebook's cost of sales in 2013 was $1.875 billion rising to $2.867 billion two years later. During that time, its sales went from $7.872 billion to $17.928 billion. A huge chunk of these companies' costs is fixed. And as we saw earlier, consumers causing costs are often not the same as customers producing revenues. This means that, ultimately, *a tech business with very high fixed costs and very low variable costs should not look to industrial firms' strategies* to achieve commercialization success, value creation or profits.

## Achieving profitability

Once we have classified our costs into fixed and variable categories, we can explore their effects on our profit. So, we're going to take a look at revenues, to see what factors affect profits other than costs. Most businesses are at some point interested in knowing the revenues necessary to just match the total costs in carrying out operations. Ultimately, firms want an indication of the total revenues or sales they need to make in order to attain the profit target they want.

The **break-even point** is the point in the operations of an enterprise when its revenues and expired costs are exactly equal. If an enterprise keeps running at this level of operations, it will make neither a profit nor a loss. We can use break-even analysis as a useful tool for visualizing future performance scenarios for a business, and this can feed into our business planning.

We can work out the break-even point using a mathematical equation. This is an equation which indicates the relationship between revenue, costs and capacity of our business. The data needed to run it are:

a) the estimated fixed costs for a future period, such as a year;

b) the estimated variable costs for the same period.

We start with this basic idea:

$$\text{Profit} = \text{Sales} - \text{Costs} = (\text{Selling price per unit} \times \text{Quantity}) - \text{Variable costs} + \text{Fixed costs})$$

If Sales = Costs, then the business is making no profit. The volume of activity where this occurs is the break-even point.

Suppose a start-up's fixed costs are estimated at £90,000, and the expected variable costs are 10 per cent of sales (S). That would mean that their break-even point is £100,000 of sales. Here's how we work it out:

$$\text{Break-even sales} = \text{Fixed costs} + \text{Variable costs}$$
$$S = £90{,}000 + 10\%S$$
$$90\%S = £90{,}000$$
$$S = £100{,}000$$

The profit and loss statement would look like Table 3.1:

**Table 3.1** Profit and loss statement

| | | |
|---|---|---|
| Sales | | £100,000 |
| Expenses: | | |
| Variable costs (£100,000 × 10%) | £10,000 | |
| Fixed costs | £90,000 | £100,000 |
| Operating profit | | 0 |

This is also shown in the graph in Figure 3.7. We can describe a business's break-even point either in terms of total sales or in terms of units of sales. For example, if the unit selling price is £50, the

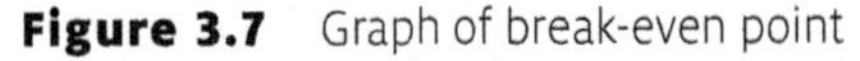

**Figure 3.7** Graph of break-even point

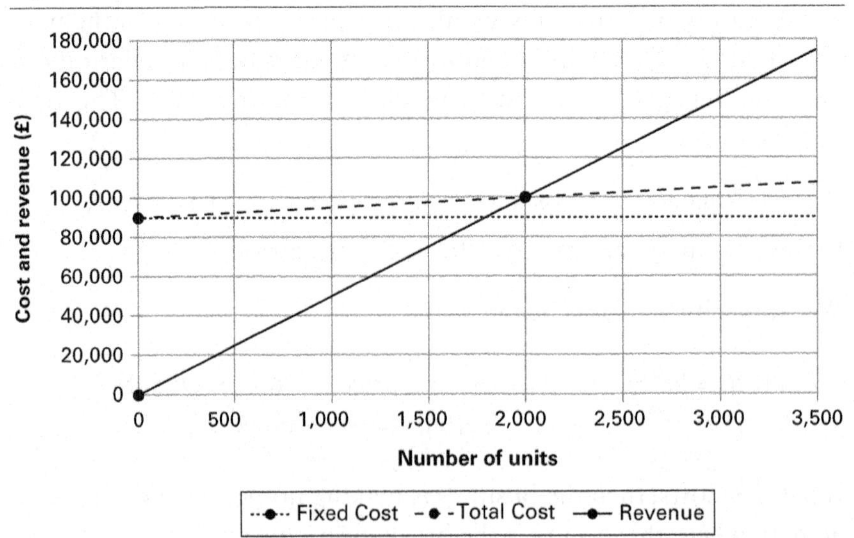

break-even point can be expressed as either £100,000 of sales, or 2,000 units (£100,000 / £50). The break-even point will then change if there are changes in the fixed costs, unit variable costs or the unit selling price.

So, as we've seen, at the break-even point, sales and costs are exactly equal. If we want to work out the sales volume we need in order to reach our desired amount of profit, we just factor the desired profit into our equation.

Let's see how that works. Consider a situation in which fixed costs are £350,000, variable costs are 20 per cent of sales, and the desired profit is £200,000. The sales volume needed to achieve the desired profit is £687,500, which we work out as shown in Table 3.2:

**Table 3.2** Calculation of sales

| Sales | = | Fixed costs | + Variable costs | + Desired profit |
|---|---|---|---|---|
| S | = | £350,000 | + 20%S | + £200,000 |
| 80%S | = | £550,000 | | |
| S | = | £687,500 | | |

If we look at it the other way around, starting with the sales figure we calculated, we can see the validity of the computation (Table 3.3):

**Table 3.3** Calculation of operating profit

| | | |
|---|---|---|
| Sales | | £687,500 |
| Expenses: | | |
| Variable costs (£687,500 × 20%) | £137,500 | |
| Fixed costs | £350,000 | £487,500 |
| Operating profit | | £200,000 |

We can work out the break-even point for an enterprise selling two or more products, if we base our calculation on a specified sales mix. As long as the sales mix is constant, it's easy to work out both the break-even point and the sales needed to achieve the desired profit.

Using total cost and total revenue calculations like this is one way of working out what it takes to break even. But this isn't always the simplest approach. Different kinds of products make for completely different use of resources, and so, different break-even points. If we focus on the singular unit, this can be a better way to home in on ways to maximize profit. When we think about costs in terms of how they behave at the unit level, this can help us make some very useful decisions. This way of doing it involves analysing contribution margin, which means we have to get to grips with fixed vs variable cost components. **Contribution margin** is simply sales revenue, less variable costs. In other words, the contribution margin represents the amount left available from sales to cover fixed costs and, ultimately, to produce a profit.

Let's look at a video game example. We might imagine that sales of physical discs are becoming increasingly irrelevant in our wireless digital world. But in fact, sales of console games in physical format remain very high. In 2015, 44 per cent of all computer and video games in the US were sold in physical form. GameStop, one of the world's largest video games retailers, made 90 per cent of its profit from physical video games in 2010. GameStop estimates that, for 2019, this will still count for 50 per cent of its earnings (Statista, nd; Makuch, 2016). It seems that video games are still being widely purchased as software burned on a physical disc, packaged in a box and shrink-wrapped with plastic.

So, suppose another video game retailer, Respawn Entertainment, releases *Titanfall 5* with the following predetermined unit cost estimates. These are based on producing and selling 25 million units in physical format (Table 3.4):

Then Respawn gets a special order from a foreign distributor, which wants to buy 2 million units at $10 each. Luckily, Respawn

**Table 3.4** Total cost per unit calculation

| | |
|---|---|
| Variable production labour, material and overhead costs | $4 |
| Fixed factory overhead cost | $10 |
| Variable selling and administrative costs | $5 |
| Fixed selling and administrative costs | $2 |
| Total costs per unit | $ 21 |

does have enough excess capacity to make an extra 2 million units. However, if it accepts the order, it will end up with special selling and administrative expenses of $500,000. On the other hand, it will have no variable selling and administrative costs at all. Is it worthwhile for Respawn to accept the order?

The unit costs we need to look at to work this out are the variable production costs. They total $4 per unit for *Titanfall 5*. Subtract that from the $10 per unit that the distributor will pay, and we get a unit contribution margin of $6. Multiply that by the total number of units they want to buy, and you get a total contribution margin of $12 million ($6 × 2 million units). This far exceeds the contract's fixed costs for Respawn of $500,000. Remember that, for this kind of analysis, we only need to look at the incremental costs of the contract. The allocated fixed costs aren't relevant, because these won't alter if Respawn goes ahead and accepts the order. It has spare capacity and does not need to incur any further fixed costs.

Suppose now that Respawn can reduce the variable production costs by $2 per unit, by outsourcing the shrink-wrapping process at a cost of $3 per unit. If it does this, Respawn will then be able to rent out part of its facilities to a local firm for $27 million per year. Should Respawn stick to shrink-wrapping the games itself, or should it outsource the process?

Let's go through the calculation. Outsourcing the shrink-wrapping is slightly more expensive than Respawn doing it themselves, giving an incremental unit cost of $1 per unit, for 25 million units. However, freeing up their space so they can rent it out would result in incremental revenues of $27 million per year. So, the incremental profit from going ahead with this plan would be $27 million – ($1 × 25 million) = $2 million. Respawn should go ahead and outsource.

The key things to think about when it comes to incremental costs are: a) whether costs differ between the alternative courses of action you have; and b) whether these costs imply future incursions. These are the only costs that are relevant for doing this kind of analysis.

## ..tribution margin in a 'winner takes all' world

Digital products have a tendency to absorb high fixed costs, both for developing them and for bringing them to market. On the other hand, their variable costs tend to be very low. This mix of cost behaviour types means that firms making digital products can pursue certain commercialization strategies which wouldn't normally be open to traditional industrial firms. Not only are cost structures skewed towards fixed costs, but the fixed costs are usually sunk – which simply means they have already been incurred and can't be recovered. The small levels of variable costs, where they exist at all, also mean firms can use highly specific pricing tactics, something which is vital when it comes to navigating fast-changing tech markets. Let's see how this plays out by looking at an illustration.

Suppose E-Holo Company has developed some software called Photon, which turns photos into 3D holographic projections. E-Holo is about to begin marketing this new product. But, it finds out it has a competitor, Holotech, which is about to launch its own software for producing holograms from photos, called TechD.

E-Holo prices Photon at \$80. It has spent \$2.8 million in development and online marketing costs over the past quarter. The software also requires initial remote support, which costs \$5 per unit.

During the first quarter, E-Holo sells 20,000 units of Photon. We can use the approach we looked at above to figure out E-Holo's profit for the quarter:

$$\text{Profit} = \text{Sales} - \text{Costs} = (\text{Selling price per unit} \times \text{Quantity}) - (\text{Variable costs} + \text{Fixed costs})$$

so,

$$\begin{aligned}\text{Profit} &= (\$80 \times 20{,}000) - [(\$5 \times 20{,}000) + \$2{,}800{,}000] \\ &= -\,\$1{,}300{,}000\end{aligned}$$

E-Holo makes a loss of \$1.3 million in the first quarter.

Now, let's look at Holotech's figures. They sell 25,000 units of their TechD package. TechD is also priced at \$80. Holotech's fixed costs during the quarter come to \$3.1 million, and its variable costs are \$4 per unit. So, for Holotech, the profit level for the first quarter is:

$$\begin{aligned}\text{Profit} &= (\$80 \times 25{,}000) - [(\$4 \times 25{,}000) + \$3{,}100{,}000] \\ &= -\ \$1{,}200{,}000\end{aligned}$$

E-Holo and Holotech incur losses during the first quarter of launch.

Then, during the next quarter, consumer interest in the product grows. E-Holo manages to sell 35,000 units of Photon. Holotech, thanks to very successful digital marketing, sells 240,000 units of TechD. Both firms keep the price the same, at $80. They both incur exactly the same variable and fixed costs during the second quarter as they did in the first. For E-Holo, then:

$$\begin{aligned}\text{E-Holo's Q2 profit} &= (\$80 \times 35{,}000) - [(\$5 \times 35{,}000) + \$2{,}800{,}000] \\ &= -\ \$175{,}000\end{aligned}$$

The company still makes a loss, but a much smaller one than in the previous quarter.

By contrast, Holotech's profit for the second quarter is:

$$\begin{aligned}\text{Holotech's Q2 profit} &= (\$80 \times 240{,}000) - [(\$4 \times 240{,}000) + \\ &\quad \$3{,}100{,}000] \\ &= -\ \$15{,}140{,}000\end{aligned}$$

The large volume of sales has produced a good profit level for Holotech, and the company has three-quarters of the consumer market for the product.

During the third quarter, customer sales rise very quickly for both firms. E-Holo sell 300,000 units of Photon, and Holotech sell 2,700,000 units of TechD. The selling prices, variable and fixed costs remain the same:

$$\begin{aligned}\text{E-Holo's Q3 profit} &= (\$80 \times 300{,}000) - [(\$5 \times 300{,}000) + \\ &\quad \$2{,}800{,}000] \\ &= \$19{,}700{,}000\end{aligned}$$

and

$$\begin{aligned}\text{Holotech's Q3 profit} &= (\$80 \times 2{,}700{,}000) - [(\$4 \times 2{,}700{,}000) + \\ &\quad \$3{,}100{,}000] \\ &= \$202{,}100{,}000\end{aligned}$$

By the third quarter, then, Holotech's profits are more than 10 times those of E-Holo, and the company has a 90 per cent market share. We can reason that, by the end of the year, Holotech's profits will be much higher, as the market grows and its market share rises even further. During the second quarter, E-Holo did not even achieve break-even, whereas Holotech had passed that level within a few days and gone on to achieve high profits. It's true that very high fixed costs were incurred to start with, as they developed and refined the product. But, once sales covered these costs, profits rose extremely quickly.

The reason for the fast increase in profits once each firm has passed the break-even point is that both companies have low variable costs and maintain a fairly high selling price per unit. This means that, once the fixed costs are covered, a large portion of the sales revenues is pure profit.

As we saw above, for both Photon and TechD, the contribution margin per unit is high. This is a key concept that is hugely useful when we want to understand the financial impact of different strategies for tech products. Let's return to the profit equation we started with:

$$\text{Profit} = \text{Sales} - \text{Costs} = (\text{Selling price per unit} \times \text{Quantity}) - (\text{Variable costs} + \text{Fixed costs})$$

We can simplify this, making it:

$$\text{Profit} = [(\text{Selling price per unit} - \text{Variable cost per unit}) \times \text{Quantity}] - \text{Fixed costs}$$

Since

$$\text{Contribution margin per unit} = \text{Selling price per unit} - \text{Variable cost per unit}$$

we can simplify again:

$$\text{Profit} = (\text{Contribution margin per unit} \times \text{Quantity}) - \text{Fixed costs}$$

Now, suppose sales in the fourth quarter are 600,000 units of Photon and 14 million of TechD. We can use this simpler equation, and work out that the profits for each company are:

$$\text{E-Holo's Q4 profit} = (\$75 \times 600{,}000) - \$2{,}800{,}000 = \$42{,}200{,}000$$

$$\text{Holotech's Q4 profit} = (\$76 \times 14{,}000{,}000) - \$3{,}100{,}000 = \$1{,}060{,}900{,}000$$

The Photon and TechD contribution margins are \$75 and \$76.

E-Holo and Holotech started out on an equal footing. But we can see how rapidly E-Holo lost both volume sales and market share. Tech-based product markets can grow very quickly, so *choosing a strategy, but then constantly reviewing it in real time, is vital* for a company to succeed. If E-Holo does not quickly put in place some effective counter-manoeuvres, it will be locked out of the market by Holotech, and TechD will **lock-in** customers. As a result, customers may find themselves faced with high switching costs. Then, even if E-Holo develops Photon further and it becomes superior to TechD, E-Holo probably won't be able to persuade customers to move over to Photon.

There are lots of examples of products which are technically weaker, but which end up dominating the market like this. Take typewriters. Back in the 1860s, type bars in typewriters tended to jam when certain letters were typed very fast, one after the other (eg 't' and 'h'). So, the QWERTY format was adopted to actually slow down typing. By the start of the 20th century, technology had advanced, but by then, both hardware and typing habits were locked into the inferior QWERTY format. There are alternative keyboard layouts, such as Dvorak and Colemak, that enable faster typing than QWERTY, but they are rarely used. The QWERTY standard is deeply locked in the market.

It was a similar story with Sega's Dreamcast, which was the most avant-garde 'net-centric' home game console available in 2000. It seemed to have a bright future. But Mr Tadashi Takezaki, who led the marketing of Dreamcast, judged that 'break-even was far too high at the time' and the company decided to stop producing Dreamcast the following year. Sega had found itself in discount wars with other console makers, which led to a situation of 'the more consoles you sell, the more you lose' (Gifford, 2013).

In 1995, Netscape had 90 per cent of the web browser market. Microsoft built its own browser, Internet Explorer (IE), and incorporated it into its Windows operating system as the default browser in every PC sold. By 2000, IE had acquired a 95 per cent market share. After that, its effectiveness as a browser lagged but for a time its market share remained very high next to alternatives. Over time, superior browsers which were costless to consumers gained the edge. So today, Chrome has a 63 per cent share vs IE's 9.7 per cent. Browser lock-in was weakened, because consumers could get easy-to-apply alternatives. Ironically, Firefox – the browser advanced by Mozilla Foundation, which was recreated from Netscape – now has a 14 per cent share of the market (Netmarketshare, 2017).

A start-up's strategy should always be geared towards learning from the market, and then growing on that basis. Marketing ploys, product features and digital marketing platforms all play a role in creating learning opportunities, which will reveal a path for forging ahead. Fast reaction and pro-active decisions are essential to growth. As part of this, it's crucial for start-ups to think about their pricing strategy. In the example above about E-Holo and Holotech, both companies could have reduced their selling price early on, and that way gained market share. It's worth bearing in mind that the selling price may tell consumers something about the product, so it's important to balance expectations of a product vis-à-vis price. Nevertheless, a lower selling price may well give you greater market traction.

Let's consider how much room E-Holo and Holotech have to revise their product prices downward. E-Holo's contribution margin is $75 for Photon, while Holotech's TechD brings in a $76 contribution. Clearly, there's plenty of room to reduce these margins. This might not be the case for manufactured products, such as the Dreamcast console, because it had high variable costs. Coupled with the deep-discount price wars, this meant Sega didn't have many options for sustaining its presence in the market. But for many digital tech products, which typically could have very high contribution margins, we can take a different approach. As we've seen, for both E-Holo and Holotech, fixed costs are initially very high. This means that there might be *pressure to achieve break-even quickly*, but this *needs to be balanced with the pursuit of market share*. If a competing product gets ahead of us with market traction, this becomes harder and harder to halt. We can end up in the same position as E-Holo: rapidly losing market share even though our profits seem to be growing handsomely.

Suppose E-Holo decides to lower the price of Photon to $70 per unit. Holotech might well follow suit and price TechD even lower, say at $65. E-Holo might then match the price of Photon, or go lower still, to say, $50. A price war would likely ensue, with both companies aiming to grow their market share, rather than getting immediate returns. How low could the companies afford to go with their product prices? Traditionally industrial firms would be very reluctant to sell below full cost (that is, the variable cost and the fixed cost allocated per unit). But sometimes it might make sense to use *a penetration strategy with a lower-than-cost price*, in order to gain market share. With tech products in particular, customers often need to experience the product before they understand its value. So, low pricing may be a great way to lure customers, who come to value the product by using it. Once people accept and value a product, the company can normalize prices so that it will eventually deliver a profit. For a start-up, this may well be the path to viability.

Because of their products' high contribution margins, E-Holo and Holotech would have no problem dipping into full cost and lowering prices for a while. If they got into a price war, though, they might end up pricing their products at exactly the same level as their variable costs. What happens then? Photon's variable cost is $5 and TechD's is $4. If the selling price is set at exactly the variable cost, that means break-even can never be achieved. This is because there would be nothing left over to cover the fixed costs. So, we'd expect both firms to show a total loss to the tune of all the fixed costs they have incurred.

If a company is going to use a '*get big fast*' strategy and try to become the biggest market player, then why not price even lower than the product's variable cost? This might be well be justified, especially when variable costs are so low, and this is usually the case for tech products. Photon and TechD could both be sold at, say, $2.

Let's take this a step further. The companies are making huge losses in the first quarter after launch anyway. So why not just grow market share by giving the product away? After all, if two products are similar, it's a company's 'staying power', during that early loss-making period, which will decide whether it captures the larger market share. You might well be anticipating the next stage in this reasoning. If we're willing to give away our product to gain a decent market share, then why not go even further, and have *negative selling prices*? Why not just pay the customer to take the product away?

Successful companies have indeed used this approach to ensure their growth, in a market which has little room for multiple players. Founded in 1997, Buy.com sold computers at below cost. The business model aimed to bring in revenues through advertising and ancillary services, such as equipment leases. The following year, its sales were $125 million. Sales more than doubled by 1999. By 2000, its revenues exceeded three-quarters of a billion dollars (Referenceforbusiness.com, nd). Similarly, PayPal quickly gained market dominance by paying customers $10 to sign up, and paying existing customers $10 for referrals. Growth immediately grew exponentially (Thiel and Masters, 2014). While not always a practical strategy, such pricing ploys have been used very successfully to speed start-up growth in markets where only a few winners can exist.

We've been looking at 'winner takes all' situations in terms of market share. It's useful to explore this in the context of specific tech products. In the example above, hologram-producing software incurs high fixed costs. As is the case for most tech start-ups, much of the fixed costs are **sunk**: they are irretrievable, so we don't need to consider them when we come to make pricing decisions. That means we have an incentive to pursue a viable 'get big fast' strategy which uses very low (or even negative) pricing.

It's important to remember a key difference between software products and industrial products, which is that software products do not necessarily show cost increases with volume changes. Imagine that, after all their research, development, coding and so on, a firm was only ever going to make one, single customized software package. Maybe E-Holo makes its hologram software exclusively for one commercial customer. This would result in the total cost for that single application being extremely high, because the fixed costs could not be spread over a large number of units. But for a tech firm like E-Holo, the variable costs of making more copies of its software product would be near zero. There would be perfect replicability of the software, without losing any quality or function. It is these unique factors, and in particular *the typically low variable costs per unit*, which make for large contribution margins for tech products. Add the fact that we shouldn't factor in our *sunk fixed costs* when it comes to pricing, *and we have a strong case for pricing low or even negatively*. With this pricing option available to us, we can pursue fast growth instead of aiming for quick and ready profits. For software products like Photon and TechD, the variable and fixed cost characteristics mean a 'get big fast' strategy makes sense. This might well include entering into price wars with competitors, alongside other tactics to gain market share.

It's clear that both the cost and the market characteristics for tech products make pursuing fast market growth very attractive, if not essential. Many companies have used this strategy, capturing vast tech market share not because their offering is superior, but because they understand how to leverage the financial circuitry of their business model.

## Summary of chapter

We have reviewed how:

- the start-up financial control loop connects up contribution, financial and progress analyses;
- knowing variable and fixed costs helps us work out financial contribution;
- break-even sales can be calculated;
- accounting intelligence helps drive smart tech start-up strategy.

## Review questions

1. What are the three elements of the tech start-up financial control loop?
2. How do variable costs differ from fixed costs in unit and total terms?
3. Show a calculation of income when a start-up is at break-even.
4. In your above example, what is the contribution margin per unit and in total?
5. What cost characteristics for a tech start-up could justify pursuing a 'get big fast' strategy?

## Further reading

Ford, M and Cummins, J (2015) *Rise of the Robots: Technology and the threat of a jobless future*, Basic Books, New York

Kelly, K (2017) *The Inevitable: Understanding the 12 technological forces that will shape our future*, Viking, New York

Ross, A (2017) *The Industries of the Future*, Simon & Schuster, New York

## References

Gifford, K (2013) Why did the Dreamcast fail? Sega's marketing veteran looks back, available at http://www.polygon.com/2013/8/7/4599588/why-did-the-dreamcast-fail-segas-marketing-veteran-looks-back [accessed 21.3.17]

Makuch, E (2016) GameStop forms publishing program to 'revolutionize' the process, available at www.gamespot.com/articles/gamestop-forms-publishing-program-to-revolutionize/1100-6438915/ [accessed 21.3.17]

Netmarketshare (2017) Desktop browser market share, available at www.netmarketshare.com/browser-market-share.aspx?qprid=0&qpcustomd=0 [accessed 6.6.17]

Referenceforbusiness.com (nd) Company profile, information, business description, history, background information on buy.com, Inc, available at www.referenceforbusiness.com/history2/24/buy-com-Inc.html [accessed 21.3.17]

Statista (nd) Breakdown of US computer and video game sales from 2009 to 2015, by delivery format, available at www.statista.com/statistics/190225/digital-and-physical-game-sales-in-the-us-since-2009/ [accessed 21.3.17]

Thiel, P and Masters, B (2014) *Zero to One: Notes on startups, or how to build the future*, Penguin Random House, New York

# Start-up financial analysis 04

In Chapter 3, we looked at the make-up of the start-up financial control loop, and discussed in accounting terms how to view the cost changes a start-up goes through as it becomes active. Now we're going to explore the second step of the loop. This involves working out how to communicate business performance in financial terms, and using this information to steer your start-up towards your vision. The goal is to ensure you get a handle on the accounting statements that help you carry out *financial analyses* of the business.

Start-ups need to communicate financial information, both to attract investors and to report on their performance as the business scales up. All businesses need to at some stage prepare sets of accounts, so they can:

- comply with reporting requirements;
- give accounting information to investors when needed;
- project the financial outcomes of different strategic scenarios.

Usually companies use a system of bookkeeping that relies on double entries. This method is meant to reflect the basic principle that financial transactions involve receiving and providing value at the same time. So, we use twin matching records, showing resource inputs and uses, work and reward, losses and gains. Double-entry bookkeeping software applications look after this for us, including creating end-user financial statements. Hence, we won't need to get into the fine details of double-entry bookkeeping here, and much of the underlying detail is irrelevant to tech entrepreneurs in any case. You just need to understand the forms of financial statements which you'll need to use to communicate and assess valuable information. So, in this chapter we'll consider:

- how we link the financial control loop to the key financial statements;
- the structure of a balance sheet and what it tells us;
- the way in which the income statement reports on profits;
- how cash flow statements allow us to monitor cash.

## The three statements that count

Let's start with the accounting equation, and the different types of financial statements we might use to give a broad picture of a start-up's financial position and performance. There are *three basic financial statements* which result from accounting processes in enterprises:

✔ balance sheet;

✔ income statement;

✔ statement of cash flows.

Most companies prepare financial statements at the end of each year (annual reports). But, a company should be able to check its own pulse at any time, and so these should always be available internally, not just at year end.

## The balance sheet

A **balance sheet** reports on a business's investing and financing activities. It shows a company's financial position at *a specific point in time* (usually the end of the accounting year). The balance sheet tells us about what the company owns – the **assets** – and what it owes to others – the **liabilities**. The gap between the two is the ownership position (ie the **stockholders' equity**). The relationship is shown in the balance sheet equation as:

Assets = Liabilities + Equity

The left side of the equation shows *what the business has*. This includes its cash, equipment, building, land, furniture, and so on. The right side of the equation shows *where these assets come from*. It tells us whether the assets are borrowed from outside parties, or contributed by the owners. Another way of visualizing this which reflects the equation is presented in Figure 4.1 which shows what portion of a company's assets the owners or non-owners can claim.

**Figure 4.1** Assets and claims on assets

| Assets | Claims on assets |
|---|---|
| What a company owns | Liabilities: What a company owes<br>Equity: Claims of owners |

As long as a company has kept good records, the accounting equation will be in balance. The left side will be equal to the right side, since every business transaction is reflected via at least two of a company's accounts (hence double-entry bookkeeping).

What exactly are assets, liabilities and equity?

- Assets are anything held by the business which will provide economic benefits in the future.
- Liabilities include the business's debts and obligations.
- Equity is any residual claim, and any financing provided, by the owners of the business. Owners only have positive financial interests in the business if the firm's assets are greater than its obligations. The equity is made up of any original **capital** invested by the owners, alongside any **reserves** coming from profits that the business has retained and reinvested. So, *equity is the sum of reserves and capital.*

We'll discuss each of these in more detail below.

When it comes to reporting certain items in a balance sheet, we have to make some assumptions. For instance, we might be able to put a pretty accurate value on our cash, but land might be more tricky to measure. The balance sheet has limitations, then, but it gives a good idea of the financial affairs of a company at a specific point in time. It comes in useful when we want to work out a company's operating performance relative to its assets, liabilities and owner's equity. The balance sheet tells us about the financial status of the firm; what it can't do is tell us about how the business arrived at that situation.

The assets in a balance sheet have some important characteristics:

- An asset has a current or probable future economic benefit. That means it could result in cash inflows, or a reduction in cash outflows, for the business. An asset might create monetary value when it is used in the operations of the business, such as when it is hired or sold.
- An economic resource only counts as an asset if the business has exclusive rights over that resource.
- Transactions or events giving rise to a business's right to the economic resource must have already taken place. Transactions or other events expected to occur in the future can't create assets today.

While the specific types of assets a firm owns will depend on the nature of its business, the type of assets that usually appear in the balance sheet include:

- non-physical resources such as cash, accounts receivable;
- physical resources such as land, building, machinery and equipment;
- intangible resources such as patents, trademarks, goodwill, copyrights;
- investments such as stocks and bonds.

A balance sheet usually lists the most liquid items (starting with cash) first, and then the least liquid items. By liquidity we mean the business's ability to meet its current obligations, and this usually implies cash and cash equivalents.

Figure 4.2 shows Amazon.com's balance sheet for the years ending 31 December 2014 and 2015.

**Figure 4.2** Amazon.com Inc: Balance sheet for the years ending 31 December 2014 and 2015

**AMAZON.COM, INC.**
**CONSOLIDATED BALANCE SHEETS**
(In millions, except per share data)

| | December 31, | |
|---|---|---|
| | **2015** | **2014** |
| **ASSETS** | | |
| Current assets: | | |
| Cash and cash equivalents | $ 15,890 | $ 14,557 |
| Marketable securities | 3,918 | 2,859 |
| Inventories | 10,243 | 8,299 |
| Accounts receivable, net and other | 6,423 | 5,612 |
| Total current assets | $ 36,474 | $ 31,327 |
| Property and equipment, net | 21,838 | 16,967 |
| Goodwill | 3,759 | 3,319 |
| Other assets | 3,373 | 2,892 |
| Total assets | $ 65,444 | $ 54,505 |
| **LIABILITIES AND STOCKHOLDERS' EQUITY** | | |
| Current liabilities: | | |
| Accounts payable | $ 20,397 | $ 16,459 |
| Accrued expenses and other | 10,384 | 9,807 |
| Unearned revenue | 3,118 | 1,823 |
| Total current liabilities | 33,899 | 28,089 |
| Long-term debt | 8,235 | 8,265 |
| Other long-term debt | 9,926 | 7,410 |
| Commitments and contingencies (Note 7) | | |
| Stockholders' equity: | | |
| Preferred stock, $0.01 par value: | | |
| Authorized shares – 500 | | |
| Issued and outstanding shares – none | – | – |
| Common stock, $0.01 par value: | | |
| Authorized shares – 5,000 | | |
| Issued shares – 494 and 488 | | |
| Outstanding shares – 471 and 465 | 5 | 5 |
| Treasury stock, at cost | (1,837) | (1,837) |
| Additional paid-in capital | 13,394 | 11,135 |
| Accumulated other comprehensive loss | (723) | (511) |
| Retained earnings | 2,545 | 1,949 |

*(continued)*

**Figure 4.2** *(Continued)*

| | | |
|---|---|---|
| Total stockholders' equity | 13,384 | 10,741 |
| Total liabilities and stockholders' equity | $ 65,444 | $ 54,505 |

*See accompanying notes to consolidated financial statements.*

**SOURCE** US Securities and Exchange Commission – Amazon.com Inc

A liability is a business's obligation arising from past events which, when the firm comes to settle it, will mean an outflow of resources. Liabilities are claims that individuals or companies, other than the owners, can make. Examples of liabilities include loans from the bank, and accounts payable.

Equity is the shareholders' interest in the assets of a business, after we've deducted its liabilities. So, it equals the assets minus the liabilities, and represents the owners' claims on the business. The funds the owners give to finance a business are claims on the business, but remember that there are two parts to this: capital and reserves. Capital is the amount the owners originally paid to the business entity. Reserves (also called retained earnings) are the owners' interests that arise from the reinvestment or retention of any past profits.

Now, let's look in more depth at these components of the balance sheet.

## Assets

There are two types of asset: current and non-current assets. *Current assets* include assets which we expect to be consumed or converted to cash within the next 12 months, and so they won't be held on a continuing basis.

### Current assets

The most common current assets are cash and cash equivalents, short-term investments and market securities, accounts receivable (called 'debtors' in the UK), inventory (called 'stock' in the UK), and prepaid expenses.

**Cash and cash equivalents** These are the most liquid assets. Some examples include currency, bank deposit accounts, negotiable instruments, money orders, and bank drafts. Cash is the ultimate measure of an organization's short-term purchasing power. The main feature of cash is that it is immediately liquid, meaning that it is instantly available purchasing power. Cash equivalents are securities with very short maturities (of up to three months), that can earn some income from interest.

**Short-term investments** These are also called marketable securities. They're different from fixed investments in that a business doesn't buy them for continuing use. They include securities bought and held for sale in the near future, to generate income from short-term price differences. Certificates of deposit (CDs), treasury bills and commercial paper are examples of short-term investments. CDs are issued by commercial banks, whereas treasury bills are issued by the government. Commercial paper is usually issued by large, high-quality companies. Companies buy these securities because they have little or no risk and have very short maturities (up to 180 days).

**Accounts receivable** This is money customers owe when the company has already provided products or services, and is waiting for payment. The business expects to receive this money usually in the next 30 to 60 days. For a company to have accounts receivable, it needs to achieve revenues in the first place.

**Inventory** Inventory represents the company's financial investments made in products it will sell to customers, or as commodities bought in order to produce products. Pure digital businesses will likely have no inventory (see Facebook's balance sheet in Figure 4.3). Where inventories exist, they may appear in three categories – the first two usually in firms that manufacture products:

- *Raw materials:* These are inventories a firm has purchased and stored for future production. The total cost of the raw materials equals the cost of bringing the product from the supplier to the company's warehouse, including its freight cost.

- *Work in process:* These are partially completed inventories – more than raw materials, but not yet ready to deliver to customers.
- *Finished goods:* These are inventories at the end of the production process, that is, fully completed products that are ready for shipment to customers. The cost of finished goods includes the cost of purchased raw materials and components used in production, the labour that assembled the products, and all of the support expenditures that helped to add value to the product.

**Prepayments** These are items where a good or service has been paid for in advance, and logged as assets, before the company has actually received, used or consumed them. A common example is insurance. These amounts will then become expenses when they are consumed.

## Non-current assets

*Non-current assets* are what firms use for continuing operations. A company would usually hold them for over a year so that it can generate wealth, rather than aim for resale. There are four main types of non-current assets: long-term investments, fixed assets (tangible and intangible) and long-term receivables.

**Long-term investments** These are investments a company holds for strategic control purposes. When a company intends to dispose of them within a year, they then become short-term investments. They may include bonds, common stock, investments in pension funds and investments in subsidiaries or affiliated companies.

**Fixed assets** These are assets a company acquires and plans to hold for more than one year, to be used for continuing operations. There are mainly two types: tangible assets and intangible assets:

- *Tangible assets:* These are assets the company owns and uses in the operation of its business, which it expects to last more than one year. There are four principal types of tangible assets:

**Figure 4.3** Facebook Inc: Consolidated balance sheets for 31 December 2014 and 2015

**FACEBOOK, INC.**
**CONSOLIDATED BALANCE SHEETS**
(In millions, except for number of shares per value)

| | December 31, 2015 | December 31, 2014 |
|---|---|---|
| **Assets** | | |
| Current Assets: | | |
| Cash and cash equivalent | $ 4,907 | $ 4,315 |
| Marketable securities | 13,527 | 6,884 |
| Accounts receivable, net of allowances for doubtful accounts of $68 and $39 as of December 31, 2015 and December 31, 2014 respectively | 2,559 | 1,678 |
| Prepaid expenses and other current assets | 659 | 513 |
| Total current assets | 21,652 | 13,390 |
| Property and equipment, net | 5,687 | 3,967 |
| Intangible assets, net | 3,246 | 3,929 |
| Goodwill | 18,026 | 17,981 |
| Other assets | 796 | 699 |
| **Total assets** | $ 49,407 | $ 39,966 |
| **Liabilities and stockholders' equity** | | |
| Current liabilities: | | |
| Accounts payable | $ 196 | $ 176 |
| Partners payable | 217 | 202 |
| Accrued expenses and other current liabilities | 1,449 | 866 |
| Deferred revenue and deposits | 56 | 66 |
| Current portion of capital lease obligations | 7 | 114 |
| Total current liabilities | 1,925 | 1,424 |
| Capital lease obligations, less current portion | 107 | 119 |
| Other liabilities | 3,157 | 2,327 |
| Total liabilities | 5,189 | 3,870 |
| Commitments and contingencies | | |

*(continued)*

**Figure 4.3** *(Continued)*

| | | |
|---|---|---|
| Stockholders' equity: | | |
| Common stock, $0.000006 par value; 5,000 million Class A shares authorized, 2,293 million 2,234 million shares issued and outstanding, including 8 million and 13 million shares subject to repurchase, as of December 31, 2015 and December 31, 2014, respectively; 4,141 million Class B shares authorized, 552 million and 563 million shares issued and outstanding, including 3 million and 6 million outstanding shares subject to repurchase, as of December 31, 2015 and December 31, 2014, respectively. | – | – |
| Additional paid-in capital | 34,886 | 30,225 |
| Accumulated other comprehensive loss | (455) | (228) |
| Retained earnings | 9,787 | 6,099 |
| Total stockholders' equity | 44,218 | 36,096 |
| **Total liabilities and stockholders' equity** | $ 49,407 | $ 39,966 |

**SOURCE** US Securities and Exchange Commission – Facebook Inc

- *Land and buildings:* This is land, factory, warehouse and building structures that the company owns.
- *Motor vehicles:* Trucks and company cars.
- *Fixtures and fittings:* Office equipment, furniture and fixtures, IT systems and hardware, and other tangible assets that support the company's operations.
- *Plant and machinery:* Plant and machinery the company uses for production and business operations.

- *Intangible assets:* These are assets we can't see, touch or physically measure. There are many kinds of intangible assets, such as patents, intellectual property, copyrights and goodwill. An intangible asset may result from a purchase, or from an expenditure of resources which will provide benefits in the future. When a business takes over another business, the acquirer generally pays more than the total value of the individual assets it acquires. This extra payment is called *goodwill*, and companies will pay it because of the skill of a workforce, or the good relationship with customers, etc. When intangible assets depreciate in value, it is called *amortization* (see below).

**Long-term receivables** Long-term receivables are debts that customers owe to the business, which they will have to repay after more than one year.

## *Liabilities*

Just like assets, we divide liabilities into current and non-current liabilities on the balance sheet. Current liabilities are what the business owes to third parties, and which it is expected to pay within a year. They include accounts payable ('creditors' in the UK), wages payable, accruals, short-term portion of loans, interest and dividends payable.

### Current liabilities

The main types of current liabilities are:

**Accounts payable** The amounts which a company owes to suppliers for goods or services it has received but hasn't yet paid for, ie the company has purchased these on credit.

**Bank notes** This represents borrowings from a commercial bank or other lenders which the company hasn't yet repaid (when repayment should take place within a year).

**Other current liabilities** These are the current liabilities that we can't class as accounts payable or bank notes. They usually come about because a company has received services it hasn't yet paid for, and this has resulted in accruals. They are different from accounts receivable in that they don't relate to purchases of traded goods. Examples of these kinds of accruals would be wages owed to a company's workers, or fees payable to outsiders for professional services or expenses such as telephone, lighting, heating, or broadband at any given point in time.

**Current portion of long-term debts** This is the amount of long-term debt that the company must pay within the year. This can include liabilities which originally had a maturity of more than one year, but which are now due for payment in less than one year.

### Non-current liabilities

Non-current liabilities are borrowings that are repayable *after a year*. They include bonds, mortgages, notes, long-term loans from financial institutions and long-term creditors.

### Equity

As we saw above, equity is simply the difference between assets and liabilities. We also call this a company's net assets, or net worth. When the business is a corporation and the owners are themselves shareholders, their equity is called shareholders' equity. Shareholders may have a different priority ranking among themselves which is shown by the use of share classes, and options. Equity is divided into two parts:

- *Capital:* The amount the owners originally paid to the business entity. The issued share capital and the paid-in capital are the total amount of capital funded by the company's shareholders. Figures 4.4 and 4.5 illustrate the assets, liabilities and equity categories for Stratasys, which is a global company providing 3D printing solutions.
- *Retained earnings:* This is the portion of company's total profits that the owners have reinvested in the business. The profits that are distributed to the shareholders are called dividends.

It is worth noting that, because we have to make certain subjective judgements and estimates when we prepare a balance sheet, the numbers on the balance sheet will reflect those estimates. For instance, to put down a figure for depreciation and amortization, we have to make an estimate about the useful life of an asset. Different calculation methods and estimates will give different measurements of how much value fixed assets have lost. Also, there are some items which don't get reported in the balance sheet, even though the business may consider them to be very valuable. The value of human

**Figure 4.4** Stratasys Ltd: Asset part of balance sheets for years ending 31 December 2014 and 2015

**STRATASYS LTD**
**CONSOLIDATED BALANCE SHEETS**
(in thousands)

| December 31 | 2015 | 2014 |
|---|---|---|
| **ASSETS** | | |
| **Current assets** | | |
| Cash and cash equivalents | $ 257,592 | $ 442,141 |
| Short-term bank deposits | 571 | 595 |
| Accounts receivable, net | 123,215 | 150,806 |
| Inventories | 123,658 | 123,385 |
| Net investment in sales-type leases | 11,704 | 8,170 |
| Pre-paid expenses | 8,469 | 7,931 |
| Deferred income taxes | - | 25,697 |
| Other current assets | 21,864 | 37,903 |
| Total current assets | 547,073 | 796,628 |
| **Non-current assets** | | |
| Goodwill | 383,853 | 1,323,502 |
| Other intangible assets, net | 252,468 | 597,903 |
| Property, plant and equipment, net | 201,934 | 157,036 |
| Net investment in sales-type leases – long-term | 17,785 | 14,822 |
| Deferred income taxes and other non-current assets | 11,243 | 9,216 |
| Total non-current assets | 867,283 | 2,102,479 |
| **Total assets** | $ 1,414,356 | $ 2,899,107 |

**SOURCE** Investors.stratasys.com

resources, the reputation of the venture capital firm with an equity stake in the start-up, and brand loyalty, are all really important for a tech start-up, but these aren't included in the balance sheet. On top of that, items on the balance sheet won't normally reflect actual market price values, and the historical cost of an asset may be wide of the mark. So, balance sheets are useful tools, but we should be aware of their limits. Now, let's look at the second key financial statement – the income statement.

**Figure 4.5** Stratasys Ltd: Liabilities and equity part of balance sheets for the years ending 31 December 2014 and 2015 (in thousands, except share data)

**STRATASYS LTD**

| LIABILITIES AND EQUITY | | 2015 | | 2014 |
|---|---|---|---|---|
| **Current liabilities** | | | | |
| Accounts payable | $ | 39,021 | $ | 37,359 |
| Short-term debt | | – | | 50,000 |
| Accrued expenses and other current liabilities | | 31,314 | | 34,514 |
| Accrued compensation and related benefits | | 34,052 | | 42,332 |
| Income taxes payable | | 11,395 | | 13,246 |
| Obligations in connection with acquisitions | | 4,636 | | 28,092 |
| Deferred revenues | | 52,309 | | 45,023 |
| Total current liabilities | | 172,727 | | 250,566 |
| **Non-current liabilities** | | | | |
| Obligations in connection with acquisitions – long-term | | 4,354 | | 26,461 |
| Deferred tax liabilities | | 16,040 | | 55,835 |
| Deferred revenues – long-term | | 7,627 | | 5,946 |
| Other non-current liabilities | | 22,428 | | 25,091 |
| Total non-current liabilities | | 50,449 | | 113,333 |
| **Total liabilities** | $ | 223,176 | $ | 363,899 |
| Commitments and contingencies (see note 10) | | | | |
| **Redeemable non-controlling interests** | | 2,379 | | 3,969 |
| **Equity** | | | | |
| Ordinary shares, NIS 0.01 nominal value, authorized 180,000 thousand shares 52,082 thousands shares and 50,923 shares issued and outstanding at December 31, 2015 and 2014, respectively | | 141 | | 139 |
| Additional paid-in capital | | 2,605,957 | | 2,568,149 |
| Accumulated other comprehensive loss | | (10,774) | | (3,674) |
| Accumulated deficits | | (1,406,706) | | (33,871) |
| Equity attributable to Stratasys Ltd | | 1,188,618 | | 2,530,770 |
| Non-controlling interests | | 183 | | 469 |
| Total equity | | 1,188,801 | | 2,531,239 |
| **Total liabilities and equity** | $ | 1,414,356 | $ | 2,899,107 |

**SOURCE** Investors.stratasys.com

## The income statement

The income statement (also called *profit and loss statement*, or the statement of operations or statement of earnings) shows an organization's income, less its expenses, *over a period of time*. This then gives us the firm's profit (or loss) figure. Remember that the balance sheet just focuses on a moment in time, not a period of time, and this is the key difference between the balance sheet and the income statement. A business can choose what period of time its income statement will cover – it can be anything from a year to a fraction of a year. Figure 4.6 shows the income statement of Amazon.com over two years to 31 December 2015.

The income statement gives us a summary of this relationship:

Revenue – Expenses = Profit

Revenue is increases in economic benefits during the accounting period covered in the income statement. This could be in the form of inflows, enhancement of assets or even decreases of liabilities that result in increases in equity. Expenses are the opposite, that is, decreases in economic benefits during the accounting period. These might be outflows, depletions of assets, or incurrence of liabilities that result in decreases in equity.

Entrepreneurs, investors and lenders (both current and potential) use the income statement to track revenues and expenses. It means *they can monitor the performance of a start-up over a period of time*. The net income or profit generated shows how well a company is using the funds it has borrowed and invested. It also means we can compare the company's performance across time-frames, or with other businesses. Naturally, this is important to investors when they are deciding how to invest.

There are two main methods of keeping track of a business's income and expenses: the cash method and the accrual method. The main difference between these two methods is in how they record transactions according to the time they were made. *The accrual method is the one we have to use for regulatory reporting*, like filing and tax reporting. When using the accrual basis of accounting, we record revenue when it is earned (eg when work is done or a product

**Figure 4.6** Amazon.com Inc: Consolidated statement of operations for the years ending 31 December 2014 and 2015

**AMAZON.COM, INC.**
**CONSOLIDATED STATEMENTS OF OPERATIONS**
(In millions, except per share data)

| | Year ended December 31 | |
|---|---|---|
| | **2015** | **2014** |
| Net product sales | $ 79,268 | $ 70,080 |
| Net service sales | 27,738 | 18,908 |
| Total net sales | 107,006 | 88,988 |
| Operating expenses (1): | | |
| Cost of sales | 71,651 | 62,752 |
| Fulfilment | 13,410 | 10,766 |
| Marketing | 5,254 | 4,332 |
| Technology and content | 12,540 | 9,275 |
| General and administrative | 1,747 | 1,552 |
| Other operating expense (income), net | 171 | 133 |
| Total operating expenses | 104,773 | 88,810 |
| Income from operations | 2,233 | 178 |
| Interest income | 50 | 39 |
| Interest expense | (459) | (210) |
| Other income (expense), net | (256) | (118) |
| Total non-operating income (expense) | (665) | (289) |
| Income (loss) before income taxes | 1,568 | (111) |
| Provision for income taxes | (950) | (167) |
| Equity-method investment activity, net of tax | (22) | 37 |
| Net income (loss) | $ 596 | $ (241) |
| Basic earnings per share | $ 1.28 | $ (0.52) |
| Diluted earnings per share | $ 1.25 | $ (0.52) |
| Weighted-average shares used in computation of earnings per share: | | |
| Basic | 467 | 462 |
| Diluted | 477 | 462 |

| (1) Includes stock-based compensation as follows: | | |
|---|---|---|
| Fulfilment | $ 482 | $ 375 |
| Marketing | 190 | 125 |
| Technology and content | 1,224 | 804 |
| General and administrative | 223 | 193 |

**SOURCE** US Securities and Exchange Commission – Amazon.com Inc

sold), and expenses when they are incurred (eg when we place an order). On the other hand, under the cash method, we count income at the time we actually receive the cash. Likewise, we record expenses at the time the cash was spent.

For instance, you might purchase material for £3,000 to make 3,000 units of a product, and add to this £3,000 of labour, all paid for in cash. If you were using the cash accounting method, then your expenses would be £6,000 (£2 per unit of the finished product). But if you were using the accrual method, your expenses would be £6,000 only if you also sold all those items during the same period. Let's say you only sold 1,000 items at £10 each. The accrual-based income would be revenues of 1,000 × £10 = £10,000, less expenses of 1,000 × £2 = £2,000 (ie the expenses only for the products you sold, not the total products you made). This would give a profit of £8,000 (as long as there were no other expenses).

Additionally, if half the sales you made were for cash, and the other half on credit, you would still record the full revenue of £10,000 for 1,000 units. This means that the amount of total sales in your income statement might end up being different from the total cash you actually received from sales. For the 2,000 items you made but didn't sell, your balance sheet (rather than your income statement) would show a value of 2,000 × £2 = £4,000. When you went on to sell these items in a future period, the revenues and matching expenses would be shown in your records when you came to work out your profit.

Small businesses often start out using cash accounting, but then switch over to the accrual method when they scale up. For tech start-ups, investors and lenders will usually want to see accruals-based financial statements, so it's best to report using this method from the outset.

The components of your income statement will vary depending on how complex your business activities are. However, most companies will always have the following elements in their income statements. In the operating section, you would have:

- *Revenue:* Revenues (or Sales or Turnover) are inflows of assets (or reductions in liabilities). They represent the monetary value of products and services that the company provided to its customers during the year. The customer either pays cash, or promises to pay in the future (in this case, we would record the amount as accounts receivable in the balance sheet).

- *Cost of goods sold:* Also referred to as cost of sales, this is the outflows of assets, or the incurrence of liabilities, that have come about as you have delivered or produced goods, provided services, or carried out any of your main business activities. We report cost of goods sold as an expense on our income statement at the time when we also report the sales revenue from the goods. The main component of a retailer's cost of goods sold is purchases. There might be other costs (such as the delivery of the good from the supplier) before the inventories are ready for sale. Goods purchased during a period are held as inventory awaiting sale at a later period.

Let's imagine how this works for a bookstore. The store buys a book from a publisher. The store records both the price of the book and the shipping costs as inventory in its balance sheet, until the book is sold. When the store sells the book, they remove it from their inventory and now record it as cost of goods sold. This is pretty simple for retailers like bookstores. For businesses that manufacture products rather than just retailing goods, the cost of goods sold is more complicated, as they have to include costs from manufacturing as well. These include things like material, direct labour and manufacturing overheads. We calculate cost of goods sold as *opening inventory* (that is, inventory at the beginning of the accounting period) plus the costs of our net *purchases* (or production costs if we are manufacturers) minus *closing inventory* (inventory at the end of the accounting period).

Tech firms often deal with digital products, and we will see this reflected in their income statement. Figure 4.7 shows Facebook Inc's income statements for the two years ending 31 December 2015.

- *Selling, general and administrative expenses (SG&A):* These are operating expenses which wouldn't count as cost of sales. They are expenses which aren't directly linked to the company's products or services but come from managing the business, or performing general and administrative activities. SG&A expenses include executives' and officers' salaries, legal expenses, payments to utilities (generally known as overhead), insurance, depreciation of office buildings and

**Figure 4.7** Facebook Inc: Consolidated income statements for years ended 31 December 2014 and 2015

## FACEBOOK, INC.
## CONSOLIDATED STATEMENTS OF INCOME
(In millions, except per share amount)

| | Year Ended December 31, | |
|---|---|---|
| | **2015** | **2014** |
| **Revenue** | $ 17,928 | $ 12,466 |
| **Costs and expenses:** | | |
| Cost of revenue | 2,867 | 2,153 |
| Research and development | 4,816 | 2,666 |
| Marketing and sales | 2,725 | 1,680 |
| General and administrative | 1,295 | 973 |
| **Total costs and expenses** | 11,703 | 7,472 |
| **Income from operations** | 6,225 | 4,994 |
| Interests and other income (expense), net | (31) | (84) |
| Income before provision for income taxes | 6,194 | 4,910 |
| Provision for income taxes | 2,506 | 1,970 |
| **Net income** | $ 3,688 | $ 2,940 |
| Less: Net income attributable to participating securities | 19 | 15 |
| **Net income attributable to Class A and Class B common stockholders** | $ 3,669 | $ 2,925 |
| **Earnings per share attributable to Class A and Class B common stockholders:** | | |
| Basic | $ 1.31 | $ 1.12 |
| Diluted | $ 1.29 | $ 1.10 |
| **Weighted average shares used to compute earnings per share attributable to Class A and Class B Common stockholders:** | | |
| Basic | 2,803 | 2,614 |
| Diluted | 2,853 | 2,664 |
| **Share-based compensation expense included in costs and expenses:** | | |
| Cost of revenue | $ 81 | $ 62 |
| Research and development | 2,350 | 1,328 |
| Marketing and sales | 320 | 249 |
| General and administrative | 218 | 198 |
| Total share-based compensation expense | $ 2,969 | $ 1,837 |

**SOURCE** US Securities and Exchange Commission – Facebook Inc equipment, stationery, supplies, sales salaries, sales commissions, advertising, freight and depreciation of sales equipment.

- *Research and development (R&D) expenses:* These are also shown in the operating section. Many industries view R&D expenses as linking directly to future revenues and profitability. Amazon's and Facebook's income statements, for example, show large R&D expenses.
- *Depreciation expense:* Remember that financial statements are based on historical cost. So, when a company purchases tangible assets and records these on the balance sheet as fixed assets, they usually value them at the historical cost, not the current one.

We expect to use our business's assets for a length of time which represents their useful economic life. At the end of an asset's useful economic life, it may have some *residual* (salvage) value – basically, what it can now be sold for. During the useful economic life of an asset, the value we give it in our balance sheet gradually reduces to the residual value. We call this reduction 'depreciation'. Every year of the asset's useful economic life, we need to note an amount of depreciation expense in our income statement. It's useful to think of depreciation as *a measure of the wearing out of the asset.* When we use accrual accounting, we also need to match a proportion of the asset's cost in being used up, against the revenue generated. If a business bought an asset – some machinery, say – and then showed its income that year as being reduced by the total cost of that asset, it would be understating earnings for that year. Likewise, it would then be overstating earnings during the following years when the machine is still being used but has already been expensed entirely in the first year of use. When we put together our financial statements for the end of each year, we have to show all depreciation claimed to date, subtracted from the original value of the asset.

Remember that a company's balance sheet (as opposed to its income statement) shows finances at a particular point in time. So, in the balance sheet, *net book value* is the difference between the original value (what we paid for our machine) and *accumulated depreciation* (the amount of wear so far). Accumulated depreciation is the total amount of depreciation expenses from the time we bought the fixed asset. Once our machine is three years old, say, it has reduced in value a little each year, and its accumulated depreciation is the total its value has lost. On our income statement, which covers a period of time, the depreciation charge is the depreciation expense calculated for the year we prepare that income statement. But in the balance sheet, the depreciation charge is the accumulated depreciation, and we deduct this from the cost of fixed assets.

We usually work out depreciation using one of two main methods: *straight line depreciation* is where the pattern of the benefits from the fixed asset is viewed as constant over time. So it wears out at an even rate, for all the years we use it. *Reducing balance depreciation*, on the other hand, assumes that most of the expected benefits from the asset are realized in the early years of its life. That is to say, it wears out more at first, but much less quickly later on.

In the non-operating section of the income statement, we will see:

- *Other revenues and expenses:* These cover revenues and gains that come from activities outside of, or peripheral to, the main business of a firm, rather than core business activities (eg rents, patents). This may also include gains and losses that are either unusual or infrequent, but not both (eg sale of securities or fixed assets).

There may be other irregular components in the income statement that we'll need to report separately, because they're not likely to happen next year. We report these after taxes. For example:

- *Discontinued operations:* This is the most common type of irregular item. Discontinued operations are when a company disposes of part of the business which is a distinct line of the overall business. We need to be able to distinguish the assets and operations of this segment from the business's other assets and operations. For tech start-ups, it's worth noting that changes like shifting the business location, stopping production temporarily, or other changes because of improvements in technology, do not count as discontinued operations.
- *Extraordinary items:* These are non-recurring material items that are significantly different from a company's typical activities. To count as extraordinary items, they have to be both unusual (abnormal) and infrequent. Examples would be unexpected natural disasters, expropriation, or prohibitions under new regulations.

- *Cumulative effect of a change in accounting principle:* There are often changes in accounting when a company decides to use new accounting principles. Any effects of these changes need to be shown in the income statement, after extraordinary items. An example would be a change in the methods we're using to work out depreciation.

Shareholders will also want to glean information from the income statement on how their investment is performing:

- *Earnings per share:* Companies need to show earnings per share on their income statements. Earnings per share is an important performance indicator that we can use to compare the earnings of companies. Earnings per share is subject to *dilution* (reduction), if it's possible that more shares will be issued in the future (we'll look at this in Chapter 5). We compute it as:

$$\text{Earnings per share} = \frac{(\text{Net income} - \text{Preferred stock dividends})}{\text{Common stock shares outstanding}}$$

Income statements are useful tools for investors and lenders – for looking at how a company has performed in the past, and how it might do in the future. But, we have to remember that they have the same weakness as balance sheets: when we prepare them, we have to use some subjective judgements and estimates. For instance, we have to make an estimate about the useful life of an asset (such as a machine), so that we can state a depreciation expense. Different depreciation methods and estimates will give different net income figures. However, investors are always going to focus on the 'bottom line' as a key indicator of a company's performance from year to year.

Finally, let's turn to the third key financial statement – the statement of cash flows.

## The statement of cash flows

The statement of cash flows shows the cash inflows and outflows of a business. It *shows the cash flows for all the operating, investing and financing activities*, and it does this *over a period of time.* It helps us to figure out the changes to other accounts which then affect the cash account on our balance sheet. The change in the cash account is usually not equal to net income. This is because the revenues of a company won't always be equal to the cash collected, and the expenses they list won't always equal cash actually paid out (see above for an example of how this can happen).

What we call cash here is basically any notes and coins in hand, as well as deposits in banks (or similar institutions) that the business can access on demand. What we call cash equivalents are highly liquid investments which the business can easily convert into cash, and only have an insignificant risk of changes of value. Businesses tend to hold cash equivalents for meeting short-term cash commitments, rather than for investment or other purposes. These have maturities often of just three months or even less from the date of acquisition. As noted earlier, examples of cash equivalents are money market funds, treasury bills and certificates of deposit (CDs). Because cash equivalents are so similar to cash, companies often put them together with cash in their statements of cash flows. Amazon's statement of cash flows for the years ending 31 December 2014 and 2015 is shown in Figure 4.8.

*Cash flow* is simply the flow of money in and out of the business – it's not the same as the profit made by the firm. It tells us how the company generated the cash flows it needed to finance its operations, and it does this by focusing on changes in the company's cash during the year. In other words, cash flow means:

Opening cash balance + Cash inflows – Cash outflows = Closing cash balance

For start-ups, cash flow statements are really useful, as they help us understand where our cash comes from and where we spend it. As we saw above, we usually use the accrual accounting method when we prepare both our balance sheet and our income statement. That means we have to match revenues with the expenses associated with generating them. But this method of accounting doesn't show us how and where we are getting our cash. This is why statements of cash flow are vital, as they provide answers to the 'how' and 'where' questions for the company as well as for investors and creditors. They give us a picture of the inflows and outflows of our cash, and don't bother with transactions that have no direct effect on cash receipts and payments.

The cash flow statement puts our changes in cash into three categories:

- operating cash flow;
- investing cash flow;
- financing cash flow.

The cash flow statement helps us to make judgements about:

- ✔ A business's ability to generate positive future cash flows, and what the timing and amounts of these might be.
- ✔ How well a business will be able to meet its obligations, pay dividends, and whether it needs external financing.
- ✔ The reasons for differences between net income and associated cash receipts and payments.
- ✔ How good a firm's financial position looks, on the basis of its cash and non-cash investing, and its financing transactions.

Net income is obviously an important measure of a company's performance. But, what it doesn't tell us much about is the company's ability to meet its obligations – ie its access to cash. This is because many revenue and expense transactions don't have any immediate effect on cash flow. So, cash flow and income are different ways of measuring performance. We should remember that the information we can glean from a cash flow statement is complementary to the information in the income statement. The cash flow statement tells us about a business's liquidity. It helps us to judge how well the company might cope with unexpected events, if it needed to do this by changing the amounts and timing of its cash flows. It's not surprising, then, that investors see the cash flow statement as a key element of information as cash is very important to the survival of a business. Businesses prefer cash in settlement for their claims. We have to pay our employees and suppliers in cash, at least partially. We need cash to make interest and dividend payments, to pay off debt as required, for capital expenditures

**Figure 4.8** Amazon.com Inc: Consolidated statement of cash flows

## AMAZON.COM, INC
## CONSOLIDATED STATEMENTS OF CASHFLOWS
(In millions)

| | Year Ended December 31 | |
|---|---|---|
| | **2015** | **2014** |
| CASH AND CASH EQUIVALENTS, BEGINNING OF PERIOD | $ 14,557 | $ 8,658 |
| OPERATING ACTIVITIES: | 596 | (241) |
| Net income (loss) | | |
| Adjustments to reconcile net income (loss) to net cash from operating activities: | | |
| Depreciation of property and equipment, including internal-use software and website development, and other amortization, including capitalized content costs | 6,281 | 4,746 |
| Stock-based compensation | 2,119 | 1,497 |
| Other operating expense (income), net | 155 | 129 |
| Losses (gains) on sale of marketable securities, net | 5 | (3) |
| Other expense (income), net | 245 | 62 |
| Deferred income taxes | 81 | (316) |
| Excess tax benefits from stock-based compensation | (119) | (6) |
| Changes in operating assets and liabilities: | | |
| Inventories | (2,187) | (1,193) |
| Accounts receivable, net and other | (1,755) | (1,039) |
| Accounts payable | 4,294 | 1,759 |
| Accrued expenses and others | 913 | 706 |
| Additions to unearned revenue | 7,401 | 4,433 |
| Amortization of previously unearned revenue | (6,109) | (3,632) |
| Net cash provided by (used in) operating activities | 11,920 | 6,842 |
| INVESTING ACTIVITIES: | | |
| Purchasing of property and equipment, including internal-use software and website development, net | (4,589) | (4,893) |
| Acquisition, net of cash acquired, and other | (795) | (979) |
| Sales and maturities of marketable securities | 3,025 | 3,349 |
| Purchases of marketable securities | (4,091) | (2,542) |
| Net cash provided by (used in) investing activities | (6,450) | (5,065) |

*(continued)*

**Figure 4.8** *(Continued)*

| | | |
|---|---|---|
| FINANCING ACTIVITIES: | | |
| Excess tax benefits from stock-based compensation | 119 | 6 |
| Proceeds from long-term debt and other | 353 | 6,359 |
| Repayments of long-term debt and other | (1,652) | (513) |
| Principle repayments of capital lease obligations | (2,462) | (1,285) |
| Principle repayments of finance lease obligations | (121) | (135) |
| Net cash provided (used in) financing activities | (3,763) | 4,432 |
| Foreign-currency effect on cash and cash equivalents | (374) | (310) |
| Net increase (decrease) in cash and cash equivalents | 1,333 | 5,899 |
| CASH AND CASH EQUIVALENTS, END OF PERIOD | | |
| SUPPLEMENTAL CASH FLOW INFORMATION: | $ 15,890 | 14,557 |
| Cash paid for interest on long-term debt | $ 325 | $ 91 |
| Cash paid on interest on capital and finance lease obligations | 153 | 86 |
| Cash paid for income taxes (net of refunds) | 273 | 177 |
| Property and equipment acquired under capital leases | 4,717 | 4,008 |
| Property and equipment acquired under build-to-suit leases | 544 | 920 |

**SOURCE** US Securities and Exchange Commission – Amazon.com Inc

on plant and equipment, and for expansion. A business might be making profits, but it could at the same time have real cash flow problems. For a start-up to be successful, it needs to know how to actively manage its cash flow. When start-ups fail, it is often not because they are not profitable but just that they can't find cash to pay claimants in time because of a lag in converting sales into cash. When a business has grown and is operating successfully, cash that comes from operating activities is a primary source for keeping a business going in the long run.

There are two methods of preparing a cash flow statement. These are called the *direct method* and the *indirect method*. When we use the direct method, we fill in a separate line item for each type of operating cash inflow and outflow. These items usually correspond to categories on our income statement. So, for example, cash we've received from our customers would correspond to the sales revenue we have put down in our income statement. But, as we saw just now, the income statement and the statement of cash flows give us different kinds of information. The income statement will show us all the sales we made to customers during the year, *whether or not* we actually collected all the cash from them during that year. Meanwhile, the statement of cash flows would just show us the amount of cash we collected during the year, whether that came from sales in the same year, the year before, or even future sales.

When we use the indirect method instead, we start out with our net income (Amazon's cash flow statement uses this method – see Figure 4.8). We then make some adjustments. We put down any non-cash changes in current accounts, as well as non-cash changes in non-current accounts. We add any depreciation expenses. Then we need to subtract any increases we've had in operating non-cash current assets. If there have been increases in operating current liabilities, we add these to the net income. We should now arrive at a figure which gives us cash flow from operating activities from net income. Finally, we put down any further adjustments from investing and financing activities.

These are the key steps to follow when you prepare a cash flow statement:

- *Cash flow from operating activities:* These are cash inflows and outflows to do with core business transactions, such as providing goods and services to customers. They tell us the effect on cash flow of all the typical and recurring transactions that show up on our income statement. Examples of operating cash inflow are when we collect payment from customers, or receive interest and dividends from investments. Cash outflows, on the other hand, would be when we pay employees and suppliers, or make payments for interest and taxes. To work out the net cash flow from operations (using the indirect method), we need to add back to the net income all depreciation, amortization, deferred tax and any unrealized gains and losses.
- *Cash flow from investing activities:* These include cash we pay when we buy long-term assets for making and selling products (such as a machine), and also cash we receive when we dispose of these assets. These long-term assets can be tangible assets such as buildings, plant and equipment, but could also be loans made by

the business. When we have purchased property, plant and equipment, made a loan to someone else, or acquired investments in other corporations, these would all count as cash outflows. Our cash inflows would come from doing the reverse, ie disposing of property, plant and equipment, collecting loans (other than the interest) and selling our investments.

- *Cash flow from financing activities:* These include cash flows from obtaining and repaying financing. If, for example, business owners issue stock to shareholders in exchange for cash and borrowings, these contributions would count as cash inflows from financing activities. The equivalent cash outflows would be when owners make payments to shareholders, such as dividends, or to repurchase their shares, as well as repaying loans (the associated interest is not included in this part).

We log any non-cash investing and financing activities in 'notes' to our financial statements. This helps to give a clearer picture of cash flows which can't be gleaned directly from the statement. We would add a note when our business had made an investment that didn't involve any cash – for example, buying property by issuing common stock. Even though no cash is paid, this transaction is not only an investing activity but also a financing activity. This is because, while acquiring property (a non-current asset) is an investing activity, issuing stock to do this counts as a financing activity. The main sections of our cash flow statement won't show transactions like this because they don't use cash. So, if we include them in a note, anyone reading the cash flow statement will get a fuller picture of our company's cash situation.

*Non-cash financing activities* may include:

- leasing to purchase an asset;
- converting debt to equity;
- exchanging non-cash assets or liabilities for other non-cash assets or liabilities;
- issuing shares in exchange for assets.

So, it's usual to add *notes* like this to our financial statements, as they can clarify and expand on the information we give in the main sections. We can use these notes for several things:

- ✔ to show the accounting principles (rules) we've used to prepare our financial statements;
- ✔ to provide detailed information about some of the items in the statements;
- ✔ in some cases, to provide alternative measures of the firm's assets and liabilities.

To help investors and others who might read our financial statements, we should present our information in a way that allows them to compare it with that from other companies. This means sticking to certain accounting standards. The two most significant sets of accounting standards and rules are the **International Financial Reporting Standards** (IFRS), which are followed by more than one hundred countries globally, and the US **Generally Accepted Accounting Principles** (GAAP). Publicly quoted firms and other companies follow standards when they issue their financial statements as annual reports. Along with financial statements and accompanying notes, annual reports include descriptions of significant events from that year, a commentary on future plans and strategies, and management's discussion and analysis of the year's results.

So how are the three financial statements we've looked at interdependent? The balance sheet shows us the combination of a business's assets and claims at a particular point in time. The cash flow statement shows the changes to cash over a period. And the income statement explains the changes over a period, tying these into the owners' claim in the balance sheet. The period of time covered in these statements is typically the business's accounting year. Given that each balance sheet tells us about a business's position at one point in time, then the income statement shows us how things have changed over a period between two balance sheets. We'll be able to see, for instance, how the business owners' claim has changed from one balance sheet to the next, as a result of trading operations. The cash flow statement also covers changes over the accounting period, but it does this differently: it explains any changes in the cash (and cash equivalent) balances between one balance sheet and the next. The financial analyses you can carry out with the three statements will help you work out how your start-up is doing vis-à-vis the business hypothesis you are pursuing.

## Summary of chapter

We have reviewed how:

- financial statements connect into the start-up financial control loop;
- a balance sheet tells us about the financial state of play at a point in time;
- an income statement reports on how profits are generated;
- the cash flow statement helps us keep track of liquidity changes.

## Review questions

1. What are the three main financial statements and how do they link to the start-up feedback loop?
2. What can you glean from the balance sheet which you cannot from the other two statements?
3. What can you observe in the income statement which you cannot from the other two statements?
4. What can you work out from the cash flow statement which you cannot from the other two statements?
5. Can you predict a start-up's future performance from the three financial statements?

## Further reading

Bamber, M and Parry, S (2014) *Accounting and Finance for Managers: A decision-making approach*, Kogan Page, London, UK

Horner, D (2017) *Accounting for Non-Accountants*, Kogan Page, London, UK

## References

Investors.stratasys.com, available at investors.stratasys.com/releasedetail.cfm?releaseid=958614 [accessed 21.3.17]

US Securities and Exchange Commission – Amazon.com Inc, available at www.sec.gov/Archives/edgar/data/1018724/000101872416000172/amzn-20151231x10k.htm#sDE44A2B31082AE97A401ABB24E2245F0 [accessed 21.3.17]

US Securities and Exchange Commission – Facebook Inc, available at www.sec.gov/Archives/edgar/data/1326801/000132680116000043/fb-12312015x10k.htm#sD6FA04C3CA64BBD51348F313A23F6C25 [accessed 21.3.17]

# Start-up progress analysis 05

We discussed the tech start-up financial control loop in Chapter 3, and identified its three steps. So far, we've explored *contribution analysis* and *financial analysis*. Now, we're going to look at the third dimension of the loop: *progress analysis*. We're interested here in how tech start-ups can monitor their progress in order to fine-tune their business pursuits, and then, how they can identify when it is time to 'pivot' the business hypothesis in a new direction. We'll see how to gauge our performance in financial terms and how we look to investors. This is what we'll cover in this chapter:

- the type of legal structure your start-up could take;
- what an auditor could say about your company's accounts;
- the main elements of the business owners' equity;
- assessing your start-up's financial performance vs business targets;
- what investors need to know about your start-up's progress.

## What type of structure is best?

Let's briefly look at the different types of start-up structures that are available to you. A start-up may begin its life as a *sole proprietorship*. This is cheap and easy to set up, but the down side is *unlimited liability*. This means that the owner is personally liable for all business debts if the business is not able to pay its liabilities. If two or more people own the start-up, then an alternative is to set it up as a *partnership*. The partners give resources to the business and divide any earnings among themselves. Most partnerships also have unlimited liability, but not all. You could really call a company any business which is set up as a sole proprietorship, or a partnership or a corporation – but in this chapter, we're going to look at accounting for companies that are incorporated.

In *corporations* (ie *formed companies*), directors are responsible for running the business, and owners only provide capital. This is different from other types of business enterprise. Owners of companies are called shareholders (or stockholders), and they are distinct from the actual business entity. They only have *limited liability* for the business's debts. Basically, *if they lose any money, it can't be more than they originally put in*. Because of this, corporations are called *limited companies*.

A limited company is formally formed and registered, and then it becomes a legal entity with the right to enter into contracts. It has the right to own, buy and sell property, and the right to sell stock. And it owns the resources, rather than its individual owners. The law treats a company as a separate person, even when it's a collection of people with a changing membership. Also, the life of an incorporated company is not related to the life of its owners and directors. For instance, if current shareholders sell their shares, the company still exists as an unchanged legal entity. This is another key feature that makes an incorporated company different from a partnership, or a business with an individual proprietor.

Some shareholders of companies have the *right to vote and to elect* members of the board of directors. The board members' responsibilities will include:

- ✔ appointing professional managers to manage the business;
- ✔ determining the company policies;
- ✔ overseeing the decisions of the management;
- ✔ protecting the interest of shareholders;
- ✔ distributing profits.

Top managers often serve on the board along with outside directors who are not part of the company's management. They might make planning decisions and develop business goals and policies.

There are two types of companies: private and public. *Public companies* have the right to offer their shares for sale to the general public. There's no limit to the number of shareholders they can have. If a public company meets the requirements of a particular stock exchange, its shares can be traded on that stock market. On the other hand, *private companies* are owned by relatively few shareholders. There's an upper limit to how many shareholders they can have. Private companies are less regulated than public ones, but there are still a few requirements they have to meet.

A company's total capital is divided into shares. A *share* just represents a unit of the shareholders' interest in the business. It's important to keep in mind that the face value of each share, and their trading value, are different. The *face* (or nominal) value is the value of a share when it is first issued. The *trading* value is the current purchase or selling price, according to the market; the market value isn't fixed like the nominal value.

There are lots of advantages to forming or 'incorporating' your company. One of the biggest is that, unlike individual proprietorships and partnerships, a company has limited liability. As we saw above, shareholders aren't personally liable for the corporation's debts. If a corporation defaults, or goes bankrupt, the most shareholders can lose is their initial investment. On top of that, shareholders can receive dividends on a regular basis. The level of dividends will be decided by the board of directors. When a company earns profit, it can either reinvest it in the business, or pay it to shareholders as a dividend. A 'formed' company like this can raise funds by issuing shares to investors, and this is something that is *particularly useful for start-ups*.

But, companies can suffer some drawbacks. Double taxation is one of these. Companies pay taxes on their profit, and separately from that, shareholders have to pay tax on any portion of the profits they get. Despite this, tax rates set by the government and tax shields on income can make it quite worthwhile to form (or incorporate) your company. There are usually low tax rates initially applicable for start-ups as well as many tax deduction incentives, because governments want to encourage small businesses and entrepreneurs. But there will be costs you'll come up against including legal costs and registration fees. It's also worth bearing in mind that incorporated companies face higher levels of regulation, compliance and accounting requirements than do partnerships and individual proprietorships. Auditing requirements could prove expensive to meet.

## The auditor's opinion

A company's managers will prepare its financial statements. It's compulsory for public companies to have their accounts *audited*, but private companies may also be audited if lenders or investors ask. *Auditors* report on whether financial statements comply with accepted accounting standards (IFRS or GAAP). The auditor will state whether an *unqualified opinion* is being given – this just means that a report does not include any material misstatements. Figure 5.1 shows the auditor's unqualified opinion on LinkedIn Corporation's financial statements as of 31 December 2015 (these are prepared

**Figure 5.1** Extract of Auditor's opinion on LinkedIn Corporation's financial statements as of 31 December 2015

**REPORT OF INDEPENDENT REGISTERED PUBLIC ACCOUNTING FIRM**

To the Board of Directors and Stockholders of
LinkedIn Corporation
Mountain View, California

We have audited the Internal control over financial reporting of LinkedIn Corporation and subsidiaries (the "Company") as of December 31, 2015, based on the criteria established in Internal Control-Integrated Framework (2013) Issued by the Committee of Sponsoring Organizations of the Treadway Commission. As described in Management's Report of Internal Control over Financial Reporting, management excluded from its assessment the Internal control over financial reporting at Lynda.com, Inc. ("Lynda.com"), which was acquired on May 14, 2015, and whose financial statement constitute 1.5% of net assets and 3.5% of net revenue of the consolidated financial statement amounts as of and for the year ended December 31, 2015. Accordingly, our audit did not include the internal control over financial reporting at Lynda.com. The Company's management is responsible for maintaining effective internal control over financial reporting and for its assessment of the effectiveness of Internal control over financial reporting, included in the accompanying Management's Report on Internal Control over Financial Reporting. Our responsibility is to express an opinion on the Company's Internal control over financial reporting based on our audit.

We conducted our audit in accordance with the standards of the Public Company Accounting Oversight Board (United States). Those standards require that we plan and perform the audit to obtain reasonable assurance about whether effective internal control over financial reporting was maintained in all material respects. Our audit included obtaining an understanding of internal control over financial reporting, assessing the risk that a material weakness exists, testing and evaluating the design and operating effectiveness of internal control based on the assessed risk, and performing such other procedures as we considered necessary in the circumstances. We believe that our audit provides a reasonable basis for our opinion...

In our opinion, the Company maintained in all respects, effective internal control over financial reporting...

Deloitte & Touche LLP
San Jose, California
February 11, 2016

**SOURCE** LinkedIn Corporation Financial Statements, 2016

according to the US Public Company Accounting Oversight Board's standards). Figure 5.2 shows a *clean opinion* for Iomart – an information technology and cloud computing company (Iomart's financial statements meet the International Financial Reporting Standards). In other words, the auditor accorded Iomart Group's financial statements a *true and fair view. Auditors don't guarantee that financial statements are correct.* They just give a professional judgement based on audit tests, which they conduct according to professional standards.

**Figure 5.2** Auditor's opinion on Iomart Group PLC's financial statements as of 31 March 2016

## INDEPENDENT AUDITOR'S REPORT TO THE MEMBERS OF IOMART GROUP PLC

We have audited the Group financial statements of iomart Group Plc for the year ended 31 March 2016 which comprise the consolidated statement of comprehensive income, the consolidated statement of financial position, the consolidated statement of cash flows, the consolidated statement of changes in equity and the related notes. The financial reporting framework that has been applied in the preparation is applicable law and International Financial Reporting Standards (IFRSs) as adopted by the European Union...

### Respective responsibilities of directors and auditor

As explained more fully in the Directors' Responsibilities Statement as set out on page 35, the directors are responsible for the preparation of the Group financial statements for being satisfied that they give a true and fair view. Our responsibility is to audit and express an opinion on the Group financial statements in accordance with applicable law and International Standards on Auditing (UK and Ireland). Those standards require us to comply with the Auditing Practices Board's Ethical Standards for Auditors.

### Scope of the audit of the financial statements

A description of the scope of an audit of financial statements is provided on the Financial Reporting Council's website at www.frc.org.uk/auditscopeukprivate.

### Opinion on financial statements

In our opinion the Group financial statements:

- give a true and fair view of the state of the Group's affairs as at 31 March 2016 and of its profit for the year then ended;
- have been properly prepared in accordance with IFRSs as adopted by the European Union; and
- have been prepared in accordance with the requirements of the Companies Act 2006.

Opinion on the other matter prescribed by the Companies Act 2006

In our opinion the information given in the Strategic Report and Director's Report for the financial year for which the Group financial statements are prepared is consistent with the Group financial statements...

Robert Hannah
Senior Statutory Auditor
For and on behalf of Grant Thornton UK LLP
Statutory Auditor, Chartered Accountants
Glasgow
6 June 2016

**SOURCE** Iomart.com, 2016

## Equity issues

Now, let's look at the various components of a business owner's equity. This will be helpful when we explore how start-ups can raise capital in Chapter 6.

*Owners' equity* is made up of capital and retained earnings – the difference between liabilities and assets. Companies refer to owners' equity as shareholders' equity (as mentioned in Chapter 4). There are several components of capital and reserves.

### *Capital*

*Capital* (also called share capital) is the amount the shareholders have directly invested; each share represents a fractional interest in the business. There are different types of shares, and their holders have different rights.

#### Ordinary shares

*Ordinary shares* are also called common stock. All formed companies must have ordinary shares, and ordinary shareholders are the *owners of the business*. We show ordinary shares on our balance sheet, and include share purchases which are always stated at the amount originally invested (ie not the market value now, but the *issue price*). After all other claims against a firm's assets have been met, the ordinary shareholders own whatever is left. That is to say, all other claims on the business have a higher priority than those of the ordinary shareholders. Ordinary *shareholders take most of the risks*, and so they expect to earn higher returns on their investments. They get these in the form of *dividends* and *capital gains*. Capital gains come from increases in the value of shares. As we've noted, the market value of the shares may well be quite different from the original issue price. If the market value is higher than the original issue price, then shareholders will earn capital gains. Ordinary shareholders are also entitled to dividends when a company finds itself with distributable profit, and it approves dividends. Usually, each share gives its holder one voting right. Corporations often have different classes of common stock with different numbers of votes per share.

## Preference shares

As well as ordinary shares, companies often issue *preference shares*. Anyone who holds preferred shares has *priority when the company pays dividends*. Preferred shareholders tend to have fixed annual dividend payments, which they are guaranteed to get. The company has to pay these dividends before it pays any to ordinary shareholders. Preferred shareholders will also have priority over ordinary shareholders if a company is liquidated, so they'll be paid back any funds before the company distributes its assets. However, the claims of creditors still take precedence over those of preferred shareholders. Also, preferred shareholders don't usually get to vote for the corporation's board of directors. There are some exceptions to this though, which are vital for tech start-ups to be aware of. We'll look at these below. Finally, preferred shares can sometimes be converted into ordinary shares, or the company might either buy them back, or cancel them under the terms of the original offer document.

## Treasury shares

When a corporation buys back its outstanding shares and holds on to them for future use, these shares are called *treasury shares*.

The treasury share reduces both cash and shareholders' equity, so in the balance sheet, we show it as a subtraction from other capital accounts. A company may want to repurchase its share for strategic reasons. It might want to 'buy out' certain groups of shareholders, to try to re-align votes according to corporate strategy. For instance, in November 2016, Facebook's board approved a buyback of shares up to $6 billion starting in early 2017. Facebook said that its buyback programme would be 'consistent with the company's capital allocation strategy of prioritizing investment to grow the business over the long term' (Bradshaw, 2016). The previous month, Alphabet Inc, Google's parent company, said it would repurchase $7,019,340,976.83 worth of its Class C stock (the amount represents 26 to the power of 'e' – a mathematical constant equal to 2.71828). It did this right after its quarterly earnings and revenues exceeded market expectations. This large buyback was in response to pressure from investors, who wanted to return some of the company's large cash pile to shareholders. Alphabet Inc had reported third-quarter earnings per share of $9.06, on revenue of $22.45 billion. They anticipated earnings of $8.63 a share on revenue of $22.05 billion (Balakrishnan, 2016).

## Share premium

Companies first issue shares when they are created. Established companies might then issue more shares to raise funds. In this case, they issue shares at a *premium*. Share premium is just the extra amount paid to the company above the *nominal* value (the value printed on the share). For instance, a company might issue shares at $17 each, even though the nominal price of the share is $1. In this case, we'd record the difference of $16 as share premium. The market value of a share is very likely to be higher than its nominal value, because over time a corporation's value goes up, as it retains profit. The market might also anticipate future profit growth, and this is then factored into the price. Share premium is also called *paid-in capital* or *capital surplus*. On the balance sheet, we show this separately below capital, but treat it like capital. Capital cannot be paid out as dividends.

## Retained earnings

As we saw in the last chapter, *retained earnings* are profits a company made in the past and either kept or reinvested in the business – they're not part of the capital owners originally put in. Retained earnings is the difference between the sum of all the profits earned since starting the business, and the sum of all dividends paid to the owners from the start. For a tech start-up, retained earnings are an important source of funds to finance expansion or other opportunities. To figure out the ending balance of retained earnings, we add together the net income earned during the period with the beginning retained earnings, then subtract any dividends distributed during the period.

### Dividends

We can view *dividends* distributed from earnings as one form of return to our shareholders, for all the capital they invested. As we've seen, we have to give priority to preferred shareholders over common shareholders when we pay out dividends. We can pay dividends in either *cash or stock*, but it's usually cash. On our income statement, dividends always appear at the bottom. Figure 5.3 shows Apple's consolidated statement of operations for the years ending 26 September 2015 and 24 September 2016. This includes the earnings per share and the dividends declared.

## Changes in shareholder equity

Shareholders' equity represents the capital that the owners invested in the company, so investors are particularly interested in this. Let's look at what can cause changes in shareholders' equity:

- ✔ share issues;
- ✔ recognition of periodic net income;
- ✔ distribution of dividends.

**Figure 5.3** Apple Inc: Consolidated statement of operations for the years ending 26 September 2015 and 24 September 2016

**CONSOLIDATED STATEMENT OF OPERATIONS**
(In millions, except number of shares which are reflected in thousands and per share amounts)

| | Year Ended | |
|---|---|---|
| | September 24, 2016 | September 26, 2015 |
| Net sales | $ 215,639 | $ 233,715 |
| Cost of sales | 131,376 | 140,089 |
| Gross margin | 84,263 | 93,626 |
| Operating expenses: | | |
| Research and development | 10,045 | 8,067 |
| Selling, general and administrative | 14,194 | 14,329 |
| Total operating expenses | 24,239 | 22,396 |
| Operating income | 60,024 | 71,230 |
| Other income/(expense) net | 1,348 | 1,285 |
| Income before provision for income taxes | 61,372 | 75,515 |
| Provision for income taxes | 15,685 | 19,121 |
| Net income | $ 45,687 | $ 53,394 |
| Earnings per share: | | |
| Basic | $ 8.35 | $ 9.28 |
| Diluted | $ 8.31 | $ 9.22 |
| Shares used in computing earnings per share: | | |
| Basic | 5,470,820 | 5,753,421 |
| Diluted | 5,500,281 | 5,793,069 |
| Cash dividends declared per share | $ 2.18 | $ 1.98 |

**SOURCE** Investor.Apple.com

We've already looked at the last two, so we'll concentrate on accounting for the first one: share issues. Take the example in the following box.

### Share issues: example

Suppose Techo Company issues 10 million shares of stock and the market price of each share is $20. So, the company raises $200 million in cash (ignoring charges). Suppose that the *par value* (which is just the original value when shares were first issued) per share is $5. That means that the issued capital equals $50 million in par value (10 million shares @ $5 each). The share premium – the extra paid on top by the new buyers – is $150 million. This is the difference between the market value of the issued shares, and the par value (or original value). Remember that, even if the shareholders decide to sell their shares to other investors, these transactions won't have any effect on Techo's balance sheet.

Existing shareholders might not like a company issuing shares, because for them, it means *losing some control*: it will increase the total number of shares outstanding. We can solve this problem by using a *rights issue*, which means we can give our existing shareholders the right to buy new shares, in proportion to the shares they already hold. Doing this allows our existing shareholders to avoid having their holdings diluted. Usually, we'd offer new shares to our existing shareholders at below the current market price.

The box below gives an example which helps to illustrate how we account for share issues.

### Accounting for share issues: example

Company Techie decides to make a one-for-seven rights issue to its existing shareholders for $5. In other words, existing shareholders get the right to buy one share at $5 for every seven shares they already hold. Imagine that company Techie has 1.4 million shares, and each share has a par value of $2. If all their existing shareholders decide to use their rights, then the company will issue 200,000 (1.4 million / 7) new shares.

The issued capital equals $400,000 at par value (200,000 shares @ $2). The share premium is $600,000 (200,000 shares @ ($5–$2)). This is the difference between the market value of the issued shares and their par value.

## Assessing progress using financials

Typically a tech start-up begins with an idea, and energy to bring it alive. If the idea is alluring enough, then some cash will hopefully follow, from the entrepreneurs themselves or from their friends and family. After that, if the start-up shows potential for success and growth, other sources of funding might emerge. These might be business angels, venture capitalists, crowdfunding investors and others. We'll go on to look at funding in the next two chapters. But for now, we're going to focus on achieving some business success, and how we can show evidence of it by using financial metrics.

Once a start-up has got its business activity going, and we can see the impact of those activities in its financial statements, we can start to do a much more detailed analysis of its performance. A start-up can use the kinds of signals we've looked at here to check on progress and fine-tune the business hypothesis. We can check metrics like active users, or acquisition costs, and they'll signal if we need a bit of a rethink – perhaps some re-jigging of the business model we're using is in order. We'll look at these metrics closely in Chapter 8. Continuously refining your business hypothesis is vital for a start-up, and you can use a whole range of signals to do this: *financial or metrics-based, as well as qualitative and even intuitive feel.* Our focus here is on the kind of refined progress analysis we can do once we've got financial statements which tell us about our economic position.

By now we've got a decent overview of all the different accounting statements, and the way they're interlinked to give us an understanding of a company's finances. So, how can we use these to dig out specific information about aspects of a business? Financial statement analysis is the key to really getting an in-depth grip on your company's performance, and how well it is progressing towards its goals. Investors also look at financial statements to make judgements about profitability, efficiency, liquidity, the success of their investment, and to check the direction the business is taking.

One approach to considering what financial statements tell us about progress is to do some 'vertical' and 'horizontal' analysis. This kind of analysis gives us a macro-level picture of any changes. In a horizontal analysis, we compare the figures in the income statement and the balance sheet *across time*. We look for year to year (or period to period) changes that relate to all the main elements in the financial statements. For example, we might look at the amount of fixed assets reported at year end, and see what that looks like as a percentage of the amount existing at the previous year end (this is sometimes called 'trend analysis'). So, if cash in the first year was $5,000,000, and in the second year it was $5,600,000, we could express the second year as 112 (that is, 112 per cent of $5,000,000).

In vertical analysis, we look at certain *numbers as percentages of broader totals* in the financial statements. We set the key figures in the accounts as 100 per cent, and then express other figures as a percentage of that 100 per cent. For instance, in the income statement, we would set the sales figure as 100 per cent, and then express every other account in the income statement as a percentage of the sales. So, if sales are, say, £2,000,000, and costs of goods sold are £900,000, then we'd express this as 45 – that is, 45 per cent of £2,000,000. In the balance sheet, we take the same approach, and state all the main categories like assets, liabilities and equity at 100 per cent. Then we can express the sub-accounts within these categories as percentages. Restating amounts as percentages like this gives us 'common size' financial statements. Analysts can then use these to compare a company's financial statements to the average in the industry. If you do find big discrepancies when you use vertical or horizontal analysis, you need to investigate them – just highlighting them is not enough! You need to figure out the reasons behind them.

Now, let's look at 'ratio analysis'. Ratio analysis is a way of understanding a business's financial position by doing some simple calculations on its figures. Ratios let us see *whether trends are improving or getting worse*. They also give us *a way of setting targets* for future performance. Financial ratios can tell us general things about a company's *financial strengths and weaknesses*, but they don't tell us anything about the causes of what we find. To do a proper assessment, we need to make sure we understand the hypothesis of the business, as well as its products, its market, the competition and the regulatory context.

When we do a ratio analysis, we might want to compare this year's ratios with those of prior years, and also with those of our competitors. This will help us assess the status of any investments made, and how the business is progressing. Using ratios to compare current performance to past performance, planned performance and competitors' performance, can help us decide what strategies to pursue. We can compare a ratio to an existing benchmark, and then make judgements about how well the business is performing. For start-ups, though, it's important to remember that benchmarks aren't fixed. They will – and should – change as circumstances change, whether operational, in the market or the industry, the economy, the regulatory environment or in technology.

To learn about specific aspects of a business, we can take a further step and categorize ratios. Each class of ratios will tell us about a particular dimension of a business's financial performance. So, when we use ratios, we'll probably want to home in on certain ones, depending on what aspect of financial progress we're interested in. We can divide financial ratios into five main categories:

- ✔ liquidity ratios;
- ✔ profitability ratios;
- ✔ investment ratios;
- ✔ efficiency ratios;
- ✔ capital structure ratios.

Let's look at each of these in a bit more depth.

## Liquidity ratios

We get **liquidity ratios** from looking at our balance sheet, and they tell us about whether a business can pay its debts. In other words, it's an indicator of the business's short-term liquidity. We can think of liquidity as a business's ability to meet its short-term obligations. Liquidity ratios also tell us something about how well the business is managing its 'working capital'. We see working capital as current assets less current liabilities. Two ratios that are often used to assess liquidity are: the current ratio and the quick ratio.

## Current ratio

The *current ratio* is the ratio of current assets to current liabilities. If current assets don't cover current liabilities, then there probably aren't enough funds to pay the creditors.

$$\text{Current ratio} = \frac{\text{Current assets}}{\text{Current liabilities}}$$

We've already seen that current assets include cash, marketable securities, accounts receivable and other current asset categories. Current liabilities include accounts payable, short-term debts, accrued liabilities and other current liabilities. If the ratio of assets to liabilities is equal to 1, then our current assets must be equal to the current liabilities. If it is below 1, then current liabilities are more than current assets, which tells us *we might have liquidity issues.*

On the other hand, if the ratio is greater than 1, it doesn't always mean the business has no liquidity problems at all. For instance, a business might have too much inventory. This would make the ratio high, but this may not be a good thing! A very high current ratio might signal to us that we've used our working capital to make wasteful investments. Too much working capital actually inhibits a business's ability to grow and prosper. This is because the extra cash could be used in better ways, such as to pay down liabilities, or even to pay dividends to shareholders. If, though, the ratio turns out to be low rather than high, this might suggest that the business can't actually afford the amount of inventory it needs to serve its customers and increase profits. So, figuring out ratios like this can be useful, but we'll also need to look for the reasons for those ratios, and perhaps also think about what would be a good ratio for our business. Below are some questions we can ask to help us identify the right ratio level for our business:

- How much cash do we need to pay the business's bills?
- What credit terms should we offer to our customers?
- What levels of finished goods inventory do we need so we can best serve our customers?
- How much raw materials do we need to make sure our production operations are efficient?

Let's consider the financials of Microsoft for 2015 and 2016 and work out some ratios (Figure 5.4).

**Figure 5.4** Microsoft: Balance sheet for the years ending 30 June 2015 and 30 June 2016.

## BALANCE SHEETS

(In millions)

| June 30, | 2016 | 2015 |
|---|---|---|
| **Assets** | | |
| Current assets: | | |
| Cash and cash equivalents | $ 6,510 | $ 5,595 |
| Short-term investments (including securities loaned of $204 and $75 ) | 106,730 | 90,931 |
| Total cash, cash equivalents, and short-term investments | 113,240 | 96,526 |
| Accounts receivable, net of allowance for doubtful accounts of $426 and $335 | 18,277 | 17,908 |
| Inventories | 2,251 | 2,902 |
| Other | 5,892 | 5,461 |
| Total current assets | $ 139,660 | $ 122,797 |
| Property and equipment, net of accumulated depreciation of $19,800 and $17,606 | 18,356 | 14,731 |
| Equity and other investments | 10,431 | 12,053 |
| Goodwill | 17,872 | 16,939 |
| Intangible assets, net | 3,733 | 4,835 |
| Other long-term assets | 3,642 | 3,117 |
| Total assets | $ 193,694 | $ 174,472 |
| **Liabilities and stockholders' equity** | | |
| Current liabilities: | | |
| Accounts payable | $ 6,898 | $ 6,591 |
| Short-term debt | 12,904 | 4,985 |
| Current portion of long-term debt | 0 | 2,499 |
| Accrued compensation | 5,264 | 5,096 |
| Income taxes | 580 | 606 |
| Short-term unearned revenue | 27,468 | 23,223 |
| Securities lending payable | 294 | 92 |
| Other | 5,949 | 6,555 |
| Total current liabilities | 59,357 | 49,647 |
| Long-term debt | 40,783 | 27,808 |
| Long-term unearned revenue | 6,441 | 2,095 |
| Deferred income taxes | 1,476 | 1,295 |
| Other long-term liabilities | 13,640 | 13,544 |
| Total liabilities | 121,697 | 94,389 |

*(continued)*

**Figure 5.4** *(Continued)*

| | | | | |
|---|---|---|---|---|
| Commodities and contingencies | | | | |
| Stockholders' equity: | | | | |
| Common stock and paid-in capital – shares authorized 24,000; outstanding 7,808 and 8,027 | | 68,178 | | 68,465 |
| Retained earnings | | 2,282 | | 9,096 |
| Accumulated and other comprehensive income | | 1,537 | | 2,522 |
| Total stockholders' equity | | 71,997 | | 80,083 |
| Total liabilities and stockholders' equity | $ | 193,694 | $ | 174,472 |

**SOURCE** Microsoft.com, 2016

## Microsoft: current ratio

Figure 5.4 shows the balance sheet for Microsoft for years ending 30 June 2015 and 30 June 2016. For the financial year 2016, total current assets for Microsoft are $139,660 (in millions) and total current liabilities are $59,357. The current ratio is.

$$\text{Current ratio} = \frac{\$139{,}660}{\$59{,}357} = 2.35$$

## Quick ratio

The *quick ratio* is also called the *acid test* ratio. It is just the ratio of very liquid assets (cash and cash equivalents, marketable securities and accounts receivable) to current liabilities.

$$\text{Quick ratio} = \frac{(\text{Cash} + \text{Cash equivalents} + \text{Accounts receivable})}{\text{Current liabilities}}$$

It can also be presented as follows:

$$\text{Quick ratio} = \frac{\text{Current assets} - \text{Inventory}}{\text{Current liabilities}}$$

The quick ratio is different from the current ratio in that it doesn't include inventory. We would use it for similar purposes to the current ratio, but it also gives us a measure of short-term liquidity. For any business with inventory, it will tell us about how well the business can meet its immediate liabilities, in a bad liquidity scenario. Inventory is a current asset, which we expect to turn into cash in less than a year. But, of course, for tech firms, like Microsoft, inventories can be expected to be low or non-existent! Since the balance sheet gives us a picture of a business at a single moment in time, the current and quick ratios worked out from the balance sheet can't tell us anything about the business's liquidity over the course of the year.

**Microsoft: quick ratio**

From Figure 5.4, Microsoft has $2,251 in inventories for year ending 2016 so the quick ratio is:

$$\text{Quick ratio} = \frac{\$139{,}660 - \$2{,}251}{\$59{,}357} = 2.31$$

## *Profitability ratios*

**Profitability ratios** indicate how profitable the business's operations are. This is a really important ratio for both the business itself and any external investors to look at, because profit is the main (though not the only) way we measure a business's success. So, these ratios mainly focus on:

- ✔ profitability the management team achieves;
- ✔ assets invested in the business;
- ✔ revenues the business generates;
- ✔ the funds that the owners have invested into the business.

There are four main profitability ratios:

- return on owners' equity (ROE);
- return on total assets (ROA);
- net profit margin;
- gross profit margin.

### Return on owners' equity (ROE)

The *return on owners' equity* (ROE) ratio compares the amount of net income to the owners' equity:

$$ROE = \frac{\text{Net income}}{\text{Owners' equity}}$$

When we work out this ratio, we might be better off using an average of the owners' equity for the year, rather than the starting or ending amount of equity, to represent the amount owners invested during the period. We get the average owners' equity simply by taking the average of the opening and closing figures for the year. Return on equity tells us how able the business is to use both borrowed funds and the owners' money effectively. It shows the residual return that's available to owners once they've covered other financing costs. We might get a high ROE figure if a business has taken a large amount of debt – this would also increase the financial risk the owners are taking.

For Microsoft we can say something quite interesting about its profitability by considering some ratios. Figure 5.5 presents the company's income statement for the year ending 30 June 2016.

**Microsoft: return on owners' equity**

From Figure 5.5, the net income for 2016 is $16,798 (in millions) and from Figure 5.4 the owner's equity is $80,083 for year ended 2015 and $71,997 for year ended 2016. Average owner's equity is, thus, $76,040 and the ROE is calculated as follows:

$$ROE = \frac{\$16{,}798}{\$76{,}040} = 0.22$$

### Return on total assets (ROA)

The *return on total assets* (ROA) ratio captures the link between a business's net income, and the amount of assets it owns. It's a really important measure of performance, because it shows us profitability

**Figure 5.5** Microsoft: Income statement for the period 1 July 2015 to 30 June 2016

**INCOME STATEMENT**

(In millions, except per share amounts)

| **Year Ended June 30,** | | **2016** |
|---|---|---|
| Revenue: | | |
| Product | $ | 61,502 |
| Service and other | | 23,818 |
| Total revenue | | 85,320 |
| Cost of revenue: | | |
| Product | | 17,880 |
| Service and other | | 14,900 |
| Total cost of revenue | | 32,780 |
| Gross Margin | | 52,540 |
| Research and development | | 11,988 |
| Sales and marketing | | 14,697 |
| General and administrative | | 4,563 |
| Impairment, integration, and restructuring | | 1,110 |
| Operating income | | 20,182 |
| Other income (expense), net | | (431) |
| Income before income taxes | | 19,751 |
| Provision for income taxes | | 2,953 |
| Net income | $ | 16,798 |
| Earnings per share: | | |
| Basic | $ | 2.12 |
| Diluted | $ | 2.10 |
| Weighted average shares outstanding: | | |
| Basic | | 7,925 |
| Diluted | | 8,013 |
| Cash dividends declared per common share | $ | 1.44 |

**SOURCE** Microsoft.com, 2016

relative to the total assets invested into a business. It helps us to assess how well a business is using its assets.

We calculate the ratio as:

$$\text{ROE} = \frac{\text{Net income}}{\text{Total assets}}$$

Here, as above, we could use the average figure for total assets instead of the closing figure. The ratio can be helpful if we want to compare rates of return with alternative investments that we might be considering. We can also use it to compare profitability across businesses, and over different time periods.

**Microsoft: return on total assets**

For Microsoft, from Figure 5.4, total assets for the year ended 2015 are $174,472 (in millions) and for the year ended 2016 they are $193,694. So, the average total assets amount to $184,083. The ROA is calculated as:

$$\text{ROA} = \frac{\$16{,}798}{\$184{,}083} = 0.0913$$

## Net profit margin

*Net profit margin* is also a key financial indicator. We work it out as follows:

$$\text{Net profit margin} = \frac{\text{Net income before interest and tax}}{\text{Sales}} \times 100\%$$

When we do this calculation, we use the net income before interest and tax. This is because it represents our profits from trading operations before we've paid for servicing any long-term finance. It also assumes that tax is a factor that the business cannot influence. This ratio basically shows how much profit the business makes, on average, on sales. It tells us about a business's pricing policies, and how well it can control costs. It might well vary from business to business, as well as from industry to industry, because of differences in competitive strategy, industry characteristics, the economic climate and product mix. So, for example, an e-tailer of branded goods may have a high net profit margin, because it has high prices and low sales volumes. In contrast, an online seller of value products may have a lower profit margin because, while its sales volumes are high, it charges pretty low prices. We can work out the reason for changes in a business's profit margin over time by looking at the relationships between specific expenses and sales.

To work out Microsoft's net profit margin, we'll need to find the interest expenses. These are included in a note to the financial statements (Figure 5.6).

**Figure 5.6** Microsoft: Notes to financial statement for year ending 30 June 2016

**NOTE 3 – OTHER INCOME (EXPENSE), NET**

The components of other income (expense), net were as follows:
(In millions)

| **Year Ended June 30,** | | **2016** |
|---|---|---|
| Dividends and interest income | $ | 903 |
| Interest expense | | (1,243) |
| Net recognized gains on investments | | 668 |
| Net losses on derivatives | | (443) |
| Net gains (losses) on foreign currency remeasurements | | (121) |
| Other | | (195) |
| Total | $ | (431) |

**SOURCE** Microsoft.com, 2016

### Microsoft: net profit margin

From Figure 5.6, interest expense is $1,243 (in millions) and from Figure 5.5, taxes are $2,953. Net income before interest and tax is thus: $16,798 – $1,243 – $2,953 = $12,602. From Figure 5.5, sales are $85,320. The net profit margin is therefore:

$$\text{Net profit margin} = \frac{\$12{,}602}{\$85{,}320} \times 100\% = 14.77\%$$

## Gross profit margin

The *gross profit margin* is the ratio of gross profit to net sales generated for the same period. Gross profit is the difference between sales and the cost of sales. For many firms this is a driver of profitability. We calculate it like this:

$$\text{Gross profit margin} = \frac{\text{Gross profit}}{\text{Net sales}} \times 100\%$$

We can also present it this way:

$$\text{Gross profit margin} = \frac{\text{Net sales revenue} - \text{Cost of sales}}{\text{Net sales}} \times 100\%$$

We can use this ratio to see the level of profits from buying or producing and selling goods, before any other expenses. If we have a high gross profit margin, this tells us that our business can make a good profit from sales, as long as we can control our overhead costs. If our gross profit percentage goes down, this could be because of lower sales prices, higher production costs, or a shift towards higher cost of sales caused by some changes in the product mix.

For Microsoft:

**Microsoft: gross profit margin**

From Figure 5.5, sales are $85,320 (in millions) and cost of sales is $32,780. The gross profit is therefore $85,320 – $32,780 = $52,540. Gross profit margin is:

$$\text{Gross profit margin} = \frac{\$52{,}540}{\$85{,}320} \times 100\% = 61.58\%$$

## *Investment ratios*

**Investment ratios** come in useful when investors want to check the returns on their investment. They tell us how the business is performing in terms of its shares, and their market value. Of course, investors benefit if the company's market value goes up. They might also get dividends from the company. Investors can use these ratios to look at both share price performance and dividend returns. There are five main types of investment ratio:

- ✔ dividend per share;
- ✔ dividend yield;
- ✔ dividend cover;
- ✔ earnings per share (EPS);
- ✔ price to earnings ratio (P/E ratio).

## Dividend per share (DPS)

This shows us the returns investors get from dividends. We calculate it like this:

$$DPS = \frac{\text{Total dividends paid for the period}}{\text{Number of shares issued}}$$

DPS tells us about an investor's cash return from holding shares in a company.

For Microsoft, we can again look to the notes in Figures 5.7 and 5.8 for the number of shares and the dividends paid.

**Figure 5.7** Microsoft: Notes to financial statement for year ending 30 June 2016

**NOTE 18 – STOCKHOLDERS' EQUITY**

Shares outstanding

Shares of common stock outstanding were as follows:

(In millions)

| Year Ended June 30, | 2016 |
|---|---|
| Balance, beginning of year | 8,027 |
| Issued | 75 |
| Repurchased | (294) |
| Balance, end of year | 7,808 |

**SOURCE** Microsoft.com, 2016

**Figure 5.8** Microsoft: Notes to financial statement for year ending 30 June 2016

**DIVIDENDS**

In fiscal year 2016, our Board of Directors declared the following dividends:

| Declaration Date | Dividend Per Share | Record Date | Total Amount | Payment Date |
|---|---|---|---|---|
| | | | (In millions) | |
| September 15, 2015 | $ 0.36 | November 19, 2015 | $ 2,868 | December 10, 2015 |
| December 2, 2015 | $ 0.36 | February 18, 2016 | $ 2,842 | March 10, 2016 |
| March 15, 2016 | $ 0.36 | May 19, 2016 | $ 2,821 | June 9, 2016 |
| June 14, 2016 | $ 0.36 | August 18, 2016 | $ 2,811 | September 8, 2016 |

**SOURCE** Microsoft.com, 2016

**Microsoft: dividend per share**

From Figure 5.8, total dividends paid for the period (in millions) are \$2,868 + \$2,842 + \$2,821 + \$2,811 = \$11,342. From Figure 5.7, total number of shares outstanding is 7,808. Dividend per share is:

$$\text{DPS} = \frac{\$11{,}342}{7{,}808} = \$1.45$$

## Dividend yield

This ratio relates the dividend an investor receives to the current market value per share. We express it as a percentage, which we work out as follows:

$$\text{Dividend yield} = \frac{\text{Annual dividends per share}}{\text{Market price per share}} \times 100\%$$

Investors can use this ratio to work out the cash returns on their investment in the company.

For Microsoft:

**Microsoft: dividend yield**

From above, the DPS is \$1.45. The market price per share of Microsoft on 30 June 2016 was \$50.72 (Nasdaq.com). So the dividend yield is calculated as:

$$\text{Dividend yield} = \frac{\$1.45}{\$50.72} \times 100\% = 2.86\%$$

## Dividend cover

This is calculated as follows:

$$\text{Dividend cover} = \frac{\text{Earnings per share (EPS)}}{\text{Dividend per share (DPS)}}$$

This tells us how many times our profit covers the actual dividends the company pays out. So, it lets us judge the company's ability to maintain its current dividend level.

**Microsoft: dividend cover**

From Figure 5.5, earnings per share for basic shares is $2.12. From the above, the DPS is $1.45. So the dividend cover is:

$$\text{Dividend cover} = \frac{\$2.12}{\$1.45} = 1.46$$

## Earnings per share (EPS)

The earnings per share ratio tells us the net income earned per share. It's another way of measuring performance, because it tells shareholders what the business has achieved for them. We calculate it like this:

$$\text{EPS} = \frac{\text{Net income}}{\text{Number of ordinary shares issued}}$$

If a business issues shares during the year, then we use the weighted average of the shares to work out this ratio. Investors will look at the trend in earnings per share when they want to assess a company's investment potential. We can use it to compare the performance and profitability of similar companies, as long as we look out for any differences in the capital structures of those companies.

For Microsoft, we can refer to the financial statement notes on EPS which state:

> Basic earnings per share (EPS) is computed based on the weighted average number of shares of common stock outstanding during the period. Diluted EPS is computed based on the weighted average number of shares of common stock plus the effect of dilutive potential common shares outstanding during the period using the treasury stock method. Dilutive potential common shares include outstanding stock options and stock awards.
>
> Microsoft.com, 2016, Note 2

The components of basic and diluted EPS are shown in Figure 5.9.

**Figure 5.9** Microsoft: Notes to financial statement for year ending 30 June 2016

| (In millions, except earnings per share) | | |
|---|---|---|
| **Year Ended June 30,** | | **2016** |
| Net income available for common shareholders (A) | $ | 16,798 |
| Weighted average outstanding shares of common stock (B) | | 7,925 |
| Dilutive effect of stock-based awards | | 88 |
| Common stock and common stock equivalents (C) | | 8,013 |
| Earnings Per Share | | |
| Basic (A/B) | $ | 2.12 |
| Diluted (A/C) | $ | 2.10 |

**SOURCE** Microsoft.com, 2016

### Microsoft: earnings per share

From Figure 5.5, net income is $16,798 (in millions). Figure 5.9 shows that the weighted average of outstanding common shares is 7,925. So, the earnings per share is:

$$\text{EPS} = \frac{\$16{,}798}{7{,}925} = \$2.12$$

## Price to earnings ratio (P/E ratio)

This is an important ratio, which tells us about the relationship between a share's market value, and our income statement. Investors use it to compare alternative investment opportunities. The equation for this ratio is:

$$\text{P/E ratio} = \frac{\text{Market price per share}}{\text{Earnings per share}}$$

We can easily get hold of market share prices for all publicly quoted companies. The book value per share is just the value of each share, if the company's assets and liabilities were sold at the figures shown in their published financial statements. The P/E ratio will often be in the financial pages of newspapers, along with the market price per share. Some investors like firms with high P/E ratios, because this shows they have high potential for growth. A low ratio, on the other hand, might suggest a slow-growing and more established company. But companies can also have low P/E ratios because they've been undervalued. These can attract investors who think the P/E will rise, so that ultimately they'll benefit from a higher stock price.

And so for Microsoft:

**Microsoft: price to earnings ratio**

The market price per share is \$50.72 and from the above, EPS is \$2.12. So, the price to earnings ratio is:

$$\text{P/E Ratio} = \frac{\$50.72}{\$2.12} = 23.93$$

## *Efficiency ratios*

**Efficiency ratios** help to show us whether a company is making good use of its resources. When we're assessing this, we tend to focus on how a company uses elements of working capital, as this tells us about how efficient the business is. So, efficiency ratios are sometimes called working capital control ratios. As we saw earlier, working capital is current assets minus current liabilities. Key elements of working capital include inventories, accounts receivable and accounts payable.

Investors use information about working capital to assess how efficiently a business operates. In general, companies may want to keep their working capital low, by keeping inventory levels and accounts receivable low, and accounts payable high. This is because it just isn't efficient to have money tied up in inventory and accounts receivable. On the other hand, low inventory levels might imply that a business can't properly satisfy customer orders. On top of that, if a business keeps its accounts receivable low, we might think this means it is reducing its credit to customers and so reducing customer growth. But, doing the opposite, and keeping creditors high by delaying payments, might harm a business's relationships with its suppliers.

The danger of keeping high levels of inventory, though, is that these could become obsolete or difficult to sell, especially when technology changes fast. Finally, if a business has high accounts receivable, this might be because customers are struggling to pay their debts. These are all things investors will look for. So, it's vital that companies effectively manage their working capital.

There are four key efficiency ratios that indicate how well a business is managing its resources:

- inventory turnover ratio;
- asset turnover ratio;
- accounts receivable collection period;
- accounts payable payment period.

## Inventory turnover ratio

The *inventory turnover ratio* looks at the cost of sales compared to the average inventory the company keeps to support those sales. We work out the average inventory by taking the average of the opening and closing inventory levels for the year. When we can't do this for any reason, we can use the closing inventory figure instead. We work out this ratio as follows:

$$\text{Inventory turnover ratio} = \frac{\text{Cost of sales}}{\text{Average inventory held}}$$

This ratio may vary from business to business, and from product to product. It helps us assess how well a company is managing its inventory - one of its most valuable assets.

We can also work out the inventory holding period:

$$\text{Inventory holding period} = \frac{\text{Average inventory held}}{\text{Cost of sales}} \times 365 \text{ days}$$

The ideal amount of inventory to hold is going to depend on factors like possible future demand, the likelihood of price rises, demand for the product, how much storage a company has, and the likelihood of future shortages. As noted, for many tech firms inventory levels can be very low or zero.

So, for Microsoft:

**Microsoft: inventory holding period**

From Figure 5.4, inventories for year ending 2015 are $2,902 (in millions) and for year ending 2016 they are $2,251. The average inventory held is:

$$\text{Average inventory held} = \frac{\$2,902 + \$2,251}{2} = \$2,576.5$$

From Figure 5.5, cost of sales is $32,780 (in millions). Inventory turnover ratio is then:

$$\text{Inventory turnover ratio} = \frac{\$32,780}{\$2,576.5} = 12.72$$

Inventory holding period is calculated as follows:

$$\text{Inventory holding period} = \frac{\$2,576.5}{\$32,780} \times 365 = 28.69 \text{ days}$$

## Asset turnover ratio

The *asset turnover ratio* compares a business's sales to its average total assets. We use it to explain how the company is using assets to drive sales. The equation for this ratio is:

$$\text{Asset turnover ratio} = \frac{\text{Sales}}{\text{Average total assets}}$$

If we can't use average asset information for any reason, we can use total assets at year end instead. Usually, a high asset turnover ratio tells us that the business is using its assets productively to generate revenue. On the other hand, a very high ratio might actually signal that the business is having problems matching its sales with available assets, because it doesn't have enough assets to do this.

**Microsoft: asset turnover ratio**

As shown above, average total assets are $184,083 (in millions). The income statement in Figure 5.5 shows that sales are $85,320. So the asset turnover ratio is:

$$\text{Asset turnover ratio} = \frac{\$85{,}320}{\$184{,}083} = 0.46$$

## Accounts receivable collection period

We use this ratio to check how long it takes, on average, for credit customers to pay their debts to the business. We calculate it as follows:

$$\text{Accounts receivable collection period} = \frac{\text{Accounts receivable}}{\text{Total credit sales}} \times 365 \text{ days}$$

The ratio gives us an average number of days that debts are outstanding. If we don't have any information about the number of sales made on credit, we can use total sales figures as an approximation.

And for Microsoft:

**Microsoft: accounts receivable collection period**

Figure 5.4 shows that accounts receivable are $18,277 (in millions). Because credit sales are not given, we can use the sales figure, $85,320 from Figure 5.5. So the accounts receivable collection period is:

$$\text{Accounts receivable collection period} = \frac{\$18{,}277}{\$85{,}320} \times 365 = 78.19 \text{ days}$$

### Accounts payable payment period

We use this ratio to see how long it takes, on average, for a business to pay its creditors. We calculate it as follows:

$$\text{Accounts payable collection period} = \frac{\text{Accounts payable}}{\text{Total credit purchases}} \times 365 \text{ days}$$

If we don't have any information about purchases the company made on credit, we can use total purchase figures as an approximation. If we don't have those figures either, then we can use cost of sales instead. Usually, it's best for a business to pay its debts slowly, but not so slowly that it loses the goodwill of its suppliers!

Again, for Microsoft:

**Microsoft: accounts payable collection period**

The balance sheet in Figure 5.4 shows that accounts payable are $6,898 (in millions). Because we don't have a figure for credit purchases, we can just use the cost of sales figure of $32,780 from Figure 5.5 instead. Accounts payable collection period is then calculated as:

$$\text{Accounts payable collection period} = \frac{\$6{,}898}{\$32{,}780} \times 365 = 76.81 \text{ days}$$

## *Capital structure ratios*

**Capital structure** ratios are the last major type of ratio that we'll look at here, and these are also called 'gearing' or 'leverage' ratios. A business can be financed either by owners' capital or debt capital. Debt capital is anything a company borrows from other parties, including loans from a bank.

Capital structure ratios can help us assess a business's strategy for financing its assets. We can also use it to measure the relative amounts of debt and equity capital a business has. If a business is highly geared (ie its borrowings are high), it is risking becoming insolvent. This is because it will be a burden to the business if it has to pay interest charges and make capital repayments. Investors are usually very keen to know a business's decisions about capital structure, as this will affect risk. There are two key gearing ratios:

- debt to equity ratio;
- interest cover ratio.

## Debt to equity ratio

We can use the *debt to equity* ratio to look at how much a business is contributing to long-term liabilities, and how much to owners' capital funds, and then compare the two. The equation for this ratio is:

$$\text{Debt to equity ratio} = \frac{\text{Long-term debt}}{\text{Owners' equity}}$$

This ratio shows us what kind of risk the company faces, given its capital structure. When the company is highly leveraged, it has to pay its debts (including principal and interest), even if it is short of cash. If a business is highly leveraged and it also has low profits, it faces even more risk.

And so, for Microsoft:

**Microsoft: debt to equity ratio**

Long-term debt is $40,783 (in millions) and owner's equity is $71,997 as shown in the balance sheet in Figure 5.4. So the debt to equity ratio is, therefore:

$$\text{Debt to equity ratio} = \frac{\$40{,}783}{\$71{,}997} = 0.57$$

## Interest cover ratio

This indicates how much profit is available to cover the interest the business needs to pay. We work it out like this:

$$\text{Interest cover ratio} = \frac{\text{Profits before interest and tax}}{\text{Interest expenses}}$$

This ratio tells us about a business's financing strategies, and lets us assess its financial risks. The lower the interest cover ratio, the higher the risk that a business can't meet its debts.

Finally, for Microsoft:

**Microsoft: interest cover ratio**

As calculated above, profit before interest and taxes is $12,602 (in millions). From Figure 5.6, interest expense is $1,243. The interest cover ratio then is:

$$\text{Interest cover ratio} = \frac{\$12{,}602}{\$1{,}243} = 10.14$$

We have considered the key financial metrics above which provide pointers to monitoring the start-up once operational activities are ongoing and business generates earnings. In the next three chapters, we'll consider further metrics which are particularly useful when the start-up is at a pre-profit stage. Here, we'll need other indicators of the start-up's progress and the signals we'll need to watch out for before we experiment with variations on the business approach or, in fact, pivot the entire business hypothesis in a different direction.

## Summary of chapter

In this chapter, we've looked at:

- what kind of legal structure a start-up might opt for;
- how auditors assess a company's accounts;
- what the components of owners' equity look like;
- how tech start-ups can monitor their financial progress;
- what financial metrics investors will want to see for an operational business.

## Review questions

1. What is the best legal structure for your tech start-up? Why?
2. What would a clean opinion from an audit of your start-up confirm?
3. What are the different types of shares you might issue for your start-up company?
4. Which financial ratios as indicators of your performance would you track to help you as your start-up grows?
5. Would you share these ratio results with your investors?

## Further reading

Bragg, SM (2012) *Business Ratios and Equations: A comprehensive guide*, Wiley, New Jersey

Ittelson, T (2009) *Financial Statements: A step-by-step guide to understanding and creating financial reports*, Career Press, New Jersey

## References

Balakrishnan, A (2016) Google parent Alphabet sees earnings, revenue beat and announces $7 billion buyback, available from www.cnbc.com/2016/10/27/google-parent-alphabet-reports-fiscal-third-quarter-q3-2016-earnings.html (27 October) [accessed 21.3.17]

Bradshaw, T (2016) Facebook unveils $6bn share buyback, available from www.ft.com/content/d8e06028-addc-11e6-9cb3-bb8207902122 (18 November) [accessed 21.3.17]

Investor.Apple.com (nd) Consolidated Statement of Operations for the years ending 26 September 2015 and 24 September 2016, available from files.shareholder.com/downloads/AAPL/4152536739x0x913905/66363059-7FB6-4710-B4A5-7ABFA14CF5E6/10-K_2016_9.24.2016_-_as_filed.pdf [accessed 21.3.17]

Iomart.com (2016) Iomart Annual Report and Accounts 2016, available from www.iomart.com/wp-content/uploads/2016/06/iomart-annual-accs_2016.pdf [accessed 21.3.17]

LinkedIn (2016) Annual Report 2016, available from s21.q4cdn.com/738564050/files/doc_financials/annual/2015/LinkedInAnnualReport_2016.PDF [accessed 21.3.17]
Microsoft.com (2016) Annual Report 2016, available from www.microsoft.com/investor/reports/ar16/index.html [accessed 21.3.17]
Nasdaq.com, Microsoft Historical Price, available at www.nasdaq.com/symbol/msft/historical [accessed 21.3.17]

# The importance of being liquid

0

Lots of start-ups fail because they just run out of cash too fast. Even if they're generating revenue, start-ups really have to keep an eye on the **runway** they have left before the cash runs out. Cash budgeting is crucial: it helps us figure out what kind of cash flow we need, with what timings, so that we can plan ahead, and ultimately stay afloat. Most post-mortems of failed start-ups find that *running out of cash is among the top five reasons for failure*. A large-scale study of start-ups that tanked found it was the second most important reason for failure (CB Insights, nd). Once a business is up and running, it needs to smooth its growth by managing cash flow properly. It should pinpoint cash shortfalls and funding needs. If a start-up isn't yet making any cash, it will have to convince investors that it really does have the potential to make a profit. In this chapter, we'll look at how start-ups can prepare and analyse cash budgets that will help them spot the timings and levels of cash they're going to need. We'll also discuss some options for financing debt. This will set us up for the next chapter where we consider funding via equity and look at valuation issues. So, we'll cover the following here:

- work out your cash inflow and outflow expectations;
- an example of a cash budget to tell us how much we'll need to raise;
- whether debt funding might work and the different options there.

## The cash budget

Sorting out a cash budget is one of the most vital tasks for a start-up. Not many businesses can survive without some form of cash planning and management. Having a cash budget means you can guide your business's activities, and be prepared for cash fluctuations. Good planning means you avoid having to wind down just because of a lack of cash. We tend to want to focus on our business: developing our product, managing customers, gauging the market, updating our investors and keeping our network current. But to keep a start-up strategy balanced, it's just as important that we think about what we owe and are owed, and look at the timing of cash coming in and going out.

Back in Chapter 4, we looked at the statement of cash flows. This is the statement that helps us see how a business's profits relate to its cash. Even though the statement shows us information about the past, we can use it as our starting point for predicting future cash flows. If you know your initial cash position, you can prepare a budget. You can then use this budget to sense how a lender or investor might react if you ask for more money, and to decide whether to pay out dividends or grow the owners' equity instead. Your cash budget will even tell you whether you should press harder for payment of your receivables, and *whether to 'lean on your payables' at the risk of upsetting suppliers.*

The whole future of your start-up depends on you really focusing on your cash budget. To set it up, you'll need to make some assumptions that will affect your projected cash at a future point in time. You might need to make guesses about how the market will grow, future revenues, how big costs could be, how your competitors will react, whether you'll get enough funding to fulfil orders, and so on. All of that thinking is part of putting together your cash budget. Preparing your cash budget is also going to force you to *confront your own levels of conservatism, optimism and intuition*. The cash budget is a picture of your business's key resource, which is effectively based on the wisdom of you and your other stakeholders. It's what will ensure your business survives and – hopefully – grows. Once you've got your cash budget sorted, you can focus on business decisions that will have an impact on cash. These will be fundamental in determining your success, whatever business strategy you're taking.

Understanding your cash flows means you *can prepare for temporary cash shortfalls* – even when they point to good performance. You can also *pinpoint longer-term cash needs*, for example, to finance capital expenditures. Then you'll have *an idea of which type of funding will be best suited* to your cash needs. Your cash budget will also reflect how risk-averse you are. You'll find out how much cash you feel you need to keep, in case certain expected inflows don't work out, or if new opportunities come up which will need cash.

If you're already operational, the revenues you expect to get will be a key part of your cash budget. So, a good place to *start is with looking at your sales* over the time period you've chosen. To figure out your starting cash position, you'll need to add sales which drive cash inflows right away, and sales made on credit in the past which are now coming due. You might have other sources of cash, for instance, from investments that are now yielding returns, or from loans giving you cash infusions. Then, you'll need to look at outflows, such as payment for supplies not on credit, and credit purchases that now need to be paid. Any salaries and wages will also make up regular cash outflows. Add to this any other expenses you have, such as paying for advertising, selling costs, administration and buying plant or equipment. Finally, include any other financing costs, such as paying off interest, and taxes.

Ultimately, your cash budget will give you a clear, structured way to show all the cash you expect to both receive and pay out. It will state the following:

The starting cash balance

*PLUS*

Collections from customers' accounts receivable, cash sales, and from other operating cash income sources such as interest received on notes receivable

*LESS*

Disbursements for purchases, wages, operational expenses and payments for rents, leases and other items

*LESS*

Other disbursements for fixed asset expenditures, long-term investments and dividends

*EQUALS*

The ending cash balance

This ending cash balance will then be the beginning cash balance for your next period of evaluation (eg the following month).

## An example

Here's an example of a start-up's cash budget preparation.

Online AustraliaMedic is using machine learning with deep algorithms to increase the medical services it can deliver online. It has been very successful at this, by giving its private patients an e-diagnostic band which they wear to help with monitoring. The device allows the company to diagnose and assess patients remotely, with information fed online. Online AustraliaMedic physicians interact with patients when needed, and give ongoing medical support. The market in Australia for online medical service provision is expanding fast. So, the company is considering further capital expenditures as set out in Table 6.1.

**Table 6.1** Online AustraliaMedic's proposed capital expenditures

| | |
|---|---|
| E-aortic monitor | $1,250,000 |
| Remote iris scanner | 600,000 |
| Respiratory sensor equipment | 400,000 |
| Web-enabled stethoscope equipment | 1,050,000 |
| Total | $3,300,000 |

The expenditures are planned for 1 October. Online AustraliaMedic's actual and estimated billings are shown in Table 6.2.

**Table 6.2** Online AustraliaMedic: Actual and estimated billings

| | |
|---|---|
| January | $ 4,400,000 |
| February | 4,700,000 |
| March | 4,800,000 |
| April | 5,000,000 |
| May | 5,200,000 |
| June | 5,300,000 |
| July (estimated) | 5,000,000 |
| August (estimated) | 5,400,000 |
| September (estimated) | 5,600,000 |
| October (estimated) | 6,000,000 |
| November (estimated) | 5,700,000 |
| December (estimated) | 5,800,000 |

Australian private insurers let patients make partial payments for using Online AustraliaMedic services. They reimburse 75 per cent of the costs, and the patients pay 25 per cent. Past experience of billing collections shows the pattern of payment by insurers and patients as set out in Table 6.3.

**Table 6.3** Online AustraliaMedic: Past billing collections

| | Insurer | Patient |
|---|---|---|
| Month of service | 30% | 20% |
| Month following service | 40 | 25 |
| Second month following service | 15 | 35 |
| Uncollectible | 15 | 20 |

Online AustraliaMedic expect this pattern of billing and collection to stay the same for the rest of the year. Table 6.4 shows their purchases over the last quarter and their plans for the last six months of the year.

**Table 6.4** Online AustraliaMedic: Past quarter and anticipated six months purchases

| | |
|---|---|
| April | $1,150,000 |
| May | 1,000,000 |
| June | 1,200,000 |
| July | 1,350,000 |
| August | 1,600,000 |
| September | 1,800,000 |
| October | 2,000,000 |
| November | 2,150,000 |
| December | 1,700,000 |

They make all their purchases on credit, and then settle the accounts payable a month later. We also know that salaries for the rest of the year will be $1,400,000 per month, plus 15 per cent of that month's billings. All salaries are paid in the month of service. For Online AustraliaMedic, the depreciation charges are $125,000 per month. The company has interest expenses of $150,000 per month, and pays for these on the last day of each quarter with a payment of $450,000. The company also gets investment income of $160,000 per month.

It has a cash balance of $230,000 on 1 July and wants to keep a minimum cash balance of 15 per cent of the current month's purchases. Online AustraliaMedic has to work out how much it should borrow to buy the new equipment it needs.

We can prepare a schedule of budgeted cash receipt for the quarter that ends 30 September as shown in Table 6.5 (figures are in thousands).

**Table 6.5** Online AustraliaMedic: Schedule of budgeted cash receipt for the quarter ending 30 September (in thousands)

| | Calculation | July | August | September |
|---|---|---|---|---|
| May: 3rd-party billings | .75 x 5200 x .15 | $585 | | |
| May: patient billings | .25 x 5200 x .35 | 455 | | |
| June: 3rd-party billings | .75 x 5300 x .15 | | $596.25 | |
| June: patient billings | .25 x 5300 x .35 | | 463.75 | |
| June: 3rd-party billings | .75 x 5300 x .40 | 1,590 | | |
| June: patient billings | .25 x 5300 x .25 | 331.25 | | |
| July: 3rd-party billings | .75 x 5000 x .15 | | | $562.5 |
| July: patient billings | .25 x 5000 x .35 | | | 437.5 |
| July: 3rd-party billings | .75 x 5000 x .40 | | 1,500 | |
| July: patient billings | .25 x 5000 x .25 | | 312.5 | |
| July: 3rd-party billings | .75 x 5000 x .30 | 1,125 | | |
| July: patient billings | .25 x 5000 x .20 | 250 | | |
| August: 3rd-party billings | .75 x 5400 x .40 | | | 1,620 |
| August: patient billings | .25 x 5400 x .25 | | | 337.5 |
| August: 3rd-party billings | .75 x 5400 x .30 | | 1,215 | |
| August: patient billings | .25 x 5400 x .20 | | 270 | |
| Sept: 3rd-party billings | .75 x 5600 x .30 | | | 1,260 |
| Sept: patient billings | .25 x 5600 x .20 | | | 280 |
| Total receipts from billings | | $4,336.25 | $4,357.5 | $4,497.5 |
| Endowment fund income | | 160 | 160 | 160 |
| Total cash receipts | | $4,496.25 | $4,517.5 | $4,657.5 |

Table 6.6 shows what the budgeted cash disbursements would look like.

**Table 6.6** Online AustraliaMedic: Budgeted cash disbursements (in thousands)

| | | July | August | September |
|---|---|---|---|---|
| Salaries: | $1,400 + (.15 × $5,000) | $2,150 | | |
| | $1,400 + (.15 × $5,400) | | $2,210 | |
| | $1,400 + (.15 × $5,600) | | | $2,240 |
| Purchases, previous month | | $1,200 | 1,350 | 1,600 |
| Interest | | | | 450 |
| Total cash disbursements | | $3,350 | $3,560 | $4,290 |

Then we can combine the two, to work out how much we should borrow, as presented in Table 6.7.

**Table 6.7** Online AustraliaMedic: Borrowing requirements on 1 October (in thousands)

| | | |
|---|---|---|
| Beginning cash balance | $ | 230 |
| Budgeted cash receipts ($4,496.25 + $4,517.5 + $4,657.5) | | 13,671.25 |
| Less budgeted cash disbursements ($3,350 + $3,560 + $4,290) | | (11,200) |
| Budgeted cash balance, 30 September | $ | 2,701.25 |
| Minimum cash balance (.15 × $1,800) | | (270) |
| Cash available for capital expenditures | $ | 2,431.25 |
| Budgeted capital expenditures | | (3,300) |
| Borrowing needed on 1 October | $ | (868.75) |

So, the company should borrow $868,750. It's useful to be able to show lenders or investors budget schedules like these. It helps them see, in a concrete way, what your plans are, and tells them you're showing foresight in planning your growth.

If Online AustraliaMedic wants to monitor its cash budget and work out deviations from expectations, it can do this with a budget vs actual **variance report**, showing actual and budgeted expenses every month (we'll look at a numerical example in Chapter 8). This type of report can have four elements that will guide your decisions. For instance, it could:

- ✔ show the budgeted amounts;
- ✔ identify the actual achievements;
- ✔ pinpoint deviations between targets and actuals;
- ✔ show the differences in percentages.

Once we work out variances, we can then consider why they came about. Are they down to events that we just couldn't have predicted? Did suppliers charge us more than we thought they would? Are we working smarter and making better use of our capacity than we thought we might? Do we need to fine-tune our forecasts?

Comparing the budget with actual outcomes lets us explore these questions, and determine pivot points in our activities. They will help strengthen our march towards growth.

## Financing your start-up with debt

Once you know your cash needs and how much runway you've got before you run out, it's time to think about how to actually get hold of cash. Any business with potential will want to find a good financing strategy. Companies can raise finance in several ways. Entrepreneurs may decide to grow a company from scratch using their own resources. This is called **bootstrapping**, and has the clear advantage of keeping the founders in full control of the business as they maintain total ownership. Naturally, they will need to have this money in the first place.

This approach will work well for businesses with low competition, and a pretty stable growth path. But for most tech start-ups this probably won't be enough. If your start-up needs to expand fast to have any chance of success in the market, you'd need to have very deep pockets indeed not to have to look at sources of funding. Chances are you'll need extensive financing for, say, carrying out R&D and knowledge development. And you'll probably know there won't be fast returns initially, and there'll be high risk. Then bootstrapping could prove to be a tough choice. But, you may not have a choice! On the plus side, if you take the bootstrapping approach you're going to be totally focused on your business, without having to worry about what investors or lenders think. And if you do really well, and reach a stage where you do need external financing, you'll look good to investors. They'll see that you navigated the start-up successfully at the outset, and they'll be able to trust that you will keep doing so with their input. In fact, many spectacularly successful entrepreneurs, from Steve Jobs to Michael Dell to Pierre Omidyar to Jeff Bezos, did just this. They bootstrapped their start-ups from scratch, and then invited in the investors (see Pilon, 2016).

You can also find sources of free cash for start-ups. There are start-up *competitions and funding contests*, but of course, entering these doesn't guarantee you'll get funded. There are also *government tax incentives*, and *grants* to promote entrepreneurship and assist start-ups. Sometimes these are focused on certain industry types or specific regions, or are meant to assist minority entrepreneurs. One drawback here is that the paperwork for applying for grants can be extensive. More of a problem is that the timing of the grant might not match up with your funding needs, and if time is of the essence, there's no guarantee you'll get the grant. If you do get funding via this route, the amount may not tally with your cash needs, and you'll probably end up burdened with reporting back to the grant-giver.

Another route might be to join an **incubator** like Idealab. Large companies, government entities, universities and venture capital firms sometimes run these. This could get you a shared space at a low monthly cost, as well as access to staff with experience and connections. If you then start to scale up, you could progress to an **accelerator**, which is what Airbnb and Dropbox did. It isn't easy to get into a top accelerator like TechStars or Y Combinator, but it can fast-track a start-up's success. These aren't the only ones – accelerators are growing in numbers globally (see the Resources section of the book). Aside from helping out with securing some cash, being part of these groups can get you invaluable knowledge and expertise, and a fast way to build up a positive network. And, if your business is progressing, you'll get interest from investors. The only downside, as we'll discuss in Chapter 7, is that you might have to give up some equity as you become bigger!

In the end, to get the cash your start-up needs, you may need to resort to *the two main sources of finance: debt and equity*. There are lots of sub-categories within these. They can be either short-term or long-term. We'll look at debt financing here, and then at equity financing in Chapter 7.

## Debt financing

Back in Chapter 4, we saw that retained profits and issuing shares are both important sources of long-term finance. But businesses will very often borrow money too, on a short- or long-term basis, and in fact, debt financing has some real merits. Aside from some lender restrictions, you decide how to spend the capital, and you stay in control of how you run your start-up. It can also be structured in a way that is very flexible and meets your start-up's specific needs and circumstances. Obviously, you do have to pay 'rent' on the money you borrow, but at least *interest on debt is tax deductible*. Of course, you'll get into trouble if you don't pay the interest you owe, or pay back the principal borrowed, meaning you could see your start-up's assets seized. What's more, you might not be able to get a loan in the first place, if your financials and credit worthiness just aren't solid. When companies do borrow money on a short-term basis, they use it to cover current cash needs. *By short-term, we mean maturities of debts being one year or less. Long-term debts are ones that are due after more than one year.* We'll go through some of the key sub-categories of short-term and long-term debt financing below.

### *Short-term debt financing*

Businesses sometimes rely on *trade credit*, which is when suppliers extend credit for purchases, usually up to 90 days. This is not always useful to tech firms with no inventory purchases. If a business doesn't have a history of ongoing operations, suppliers might not want to extend trade credit until a relationship is firmed up and the start-up has made some on-time payments. So, this can be an obstacle for start-ups. But, there are several other types of short-term debt financing you can use instead. Five important ones are:

- bank and other loans;
- accounts receivable financing;
- factoring;
- inventory financing;
- leasing.

## Loans

Bank loans and arranged overdrafts are among the most common ways that start-ups raise money. These are flexible and usually fast ways of financing your cash needs. The terms that banks offer will vary and the interest they charge will depend on the business as well as the general economic environment. *Overdrafts* and *short-term loans* will typically be linked to working cash flow. The interest charges for these will be higher than for longer-term loans, where repayment follows a defined schedule with credit offered gradually receding. We might use a loan to finance working capital when we have a pretty much continuous need as our business grows. This means that the loan is really *intermediate* – usually one to three years, but sometimes up to five years. In general, the rate of interest on short-term loans or bank overdrafts will be higher than on intermediate or long-term loans. While we might use intermediate loans for working capital, we can also use them for some asset categories, such as computer equipment or machinery. These *provide collateral security for the loan.* Often, personal property is used as collateral, instead of or as well as assets. Alongside financing working capital or assets over the short/intermediate term, we might need a long-term loan, for example to buy a property for the business. Banks will usually look at a ten-year period for these sorts of loans, with a defined repayment schedule (see below).

For any loan, you will need to say how you're going to repay the money. When you apply to a bank for money, you'll have to show cash budgets and marketing plans, to back up the business idea. Loans are generally more suited to business models that show ready revenue generation and profitability. This may not be the case for your tech start-up. Remember, the bank will look at your cash flow projections, balance sheet and income statement; it'll be interested in your current level of borrowings, net worth and profitability. It will check your ratios to judge your liquidity, efficiency, profitability, investment returns and capital structure – all the elements we went through in Chapter 5.

## Accounts receivable financing

This is when you use part or all of *accounts receivable* as collateral for short-term loans. Banks won't accept all invoices as collateral, as you might have customers with low credit ratings. If customers who bought on credit pay slowly, but your business needs working capital to grow faster, then you can use this form of lending. It means that a percentage of the accounts receivable value is released to the business with speed. The level of finance credit goes up as sales grow. Companies that offer this form of financing will have charges such as set fees (including exit fees), notice periods and maybe also audit requirements. A start-up might be able to get, say, 85 per cent of invoices upfront, and once the customer pays the invoice, more debtor financing will come through with the remaining 15 per cent, less any fee.

## Factoring

A business can choose to sell specific invoices at a discount to a bank, or to an independent *factoring* company. The company or bank will then make a cash payment to the business straight away. After that, invoiced customers owe their debt to that company or bank, rather than to the business. This type of financing can turn out to be more expensive than getting a loan. For instance, the factoring company may buy the accounts receivable at only 90 per cent face value. The whole process involves three parties: the business start-up that sells its accounts receivable; the factor ie the bank or a factoring company that buys the receivables; and the debtor who still has to pay the full value of their original invoice to the factor.

## Inventory financing

This is when a company uses its *inventory* as collateral for short-term loans. Usually, raw materials and finished goods would be used as collateral to finance the business. Inventory can lose value over time, so compared to accounts receivable financing, this type may prove more expensive. If your inventory has got quite old, you might not find a lender at all. Many tech firms have no inventory, so this form of finance would not be an option.

### Leasing

This is when a finance company purchases an asset, and then *leases* it back to the start-up for a monthly fee. The start-up has the option to buy the asset at an agreed time. This is a primary source of financing for start-ups when the bank won't lend directly, but it can be more expensive than a loan. From a tax perspective, though, leasing can be a wise move. This is because the leasing costs can be expensed in their entirety, but if you bought the same equipment with a bank loan, it would limit what you could claim as tax deductible and depreciation expenses.

## *Longer-term debt financing*

Start-ups usually need longer-term financing, to kick-start and sustain the business on a balanced trajectory of growth, and to scale up. Two main channels for funding through long-term debt are:

- long-term loans;
- bonds.

### Long-term loans

This is the most common form of financing, for periods of five to ten years. These *long-term loans* usually have fixed maturity dates and fixed interest rates. A start-up would repay this kind of loan in monthly or quarterly instalments, which cover principal and interest. A bank debt doesn't dilute ownership, and doesn't interfere in how you run the business to any great degree. But, you'd need to look out for important stipulations from the bank, especially around reporting requirements. Banks often include **restrictive covenants** on short- or long-term loans, so that your business has to make payments on the loan before other discretionary payouts such as dividends. You'll probably also need to provide a personal guarantee, though for some start-ups, government institutions may act as guarantors. You should also think about how investors might view this kind of financing. *If a start-up has a long-term loan on its balance sheet, this is a liability.* Investors will know that loan repayments will get prioritized over other payouts by the business. If a potential investor sees the loan as paying for the start-up's past growth, this might put them off giving funding for the business's future while the debt exists. Still, a long-term loan, if you can get one, can enable a start-up to grow fast, while keeping control of how you run the business. Just bear in mind that not all start-ups will have this option.

### Bonds and asset-based loans

With a bond certificate, the borrower agrees to pay interest on the debt over a period of time, then repays the principal later. *Bonds* are often marketable, and are sold to the public through a centralized authority. They are usually secured by some collateral. Individuals, companies, and institutions can buy and sell bonds. *Asset-based loans* come from finance companies, rather than banks, and involve funding back-up by collateral such as inventory, stock or other assets. Start-ups don't usually have the opportunity to use this form of debt.

## Summary of chapter

We've looked at:

- how to prepare a cash budget to tell you about your financing requirements;
- how debt financing works and different options for the short and long term;
- the relative costs of using different debt finance options.

## Review questions

1. What do you need to know to work out your cash needs?
2. Describe three ways of financing your start-up.
3. What short-term debt financing options are there for your start-up as it grows?
4. How does your cash budget reflect how risk-averse you are?
5. What are three drawbacks of debt financing for a tech start-up?

## Further reading

Jury, T (2012) *Cash Flow Analysis and Forecasting: The definitive guide to understanding and using published cash flow data*, Wiley, UK

Tiffin, R (2014) *Executive Finance and Strategy: How to understand and use financial information to set strategic goals*, Kogan Page, UK

## References

CB Insights (nd), The top 20 reasons startups fail, available from www.cbinsights.com/research-reports/The-20-Reasons-Startups-Fail.pdf [accessed 21.3.17]

Pilon, A (2016) Don't Have Money? 17 entrepreneurs who bootstrapped their start-ups from nothing, available at https://smallbiztrends.com/2016/03/entrepreneurs-who-bootstrapped.html [accessed 21.3.17]

# What's it worth to you?

07

An alternative to debt finance is equity financing. This is when a start-up issues shares of its stock in exchange for money. By issuing shares, you are basically giving up part of the business. This means you lose full ownership, and so won't have total autonomy when it comes to making decisions. Raising venture capital can take a huge amount of time and effort. If you disagree with your investors about company strategy, you might have to cash out and leave the start-up you created. Why then would you even consider equity financing? Because, despite the risk, there are real pluses. We discuss the pluses of funding via equity and the different ways of structuring this. We'll also see how you can value your start-up and we look at the all-important 'term sheet'. Finally, we'll consider the new wonder of crowdfunding. So, we'll cover the following here:

- why equity financing, and the different sources and forms it can take;
- how to work out the ownership share you'll give away;
- term sheets are what you desire – but what to watch out for;
- is crowdfunding a good idea?

## Equity financing

Giving up part of what you've built might not sound right. You end up with a smaller share of your company than when you started and you give up decision rights. You could even be asked to leave your start-up. Some tech start-up founders who got fired from their companies include: Travis Kalanick (Uber), Andrew Mason (Groupon), Noah Glass (Twitter), Jerry Yang (Yahoo!), Martin Eberhard (Tesla) and Eduardo Saverin (Facebook). You could just be philosophical and say 'Knowing the limits of one's ability and understanding when it is best for the organization to have another assume power is perhaps the greatest quality any leader can possess' (Solovic, 2015) – but still! New equity owners can force decisions you disagree with too. Take for instance, Steve Jobs, co-founder of Apple Inc, who left his company in 1985. John Sculley, then CEO of the company, explained how:

> Steve came to me and he said, 'I want to drop the price of the Macintosh and I want to move the advertising, shift a large portion of it away from the Apple 2 over to the Mac.'
>
> I said, 'Steve, it's not going to make any difference. The reason the Mac is not selling has nothing to do with the price or with the advertising. If you do that, we risk throwing the company into a loss.' And he just totally disagreed with me.
>
> And so I said, 'Well, I'm gonna go to the board'. And he said, 'I don't believe you'll do it.' And I said: '*Watch me.*'
>
> … Apple vice chairman Mike Markkula was assigned to study the issue and present a report. 'Seven or eight days later, he came back to the board and said, "I agree with John, I don't agree with Steve".'
>
> Lane, 2013

Soon afterwards, Jobs left and founded NeXT – only to return to Apple 12 years later as CEO when Apple merged with NeXT. But there is a bright side of equity financing – first, if your start-up fails, you will not owe anyone any money. Second, you won't be paying interest on a debt, so you'll have more money to nurture your start-up. Third, investors in your company might actually give you some excellent guidance. Your success is their success. They will share their wisdom with you, and they might have deep experience in the industry. They can also open up valuable networks to you.

Prior to any external funding, you might have got money from family and friends to kick-start your business venture. But their pockets may not be deep enough to finance the next stage of the business's growth. After that, if your business is fundable, it will attract investors who seek high risk for high return potential. Some investors are individuals – **angel investors** – who tend to be interested in specific industries, including tech. Because angels are usually wealthy individuals with their own reasons for investing, they'll be looking for a whole range of different things but will always want an equity stake in your business. An angel invests at an early stage (the **seed** stage) and might want to play quite an active role in your start-up, or just provide capital as a sleeping partner. They will *typically invest less than venture capitalists* who manage the pooled money of other investors. The initial seed round in the US averages $1.14 million, with the median being $625,000 (Teare and Glasner, 2016). In the UK, angels will tend to invest about £42,000 on average per company, but investments can range in size and often will go to £250,000 with 'super angels' investing more (Jee, 2017). In the USA, the amounts could go to a few million dollars. Why do they invest? Probably both for love of entrepreneurship and love of money!

Angels will want very high returns from investing because of the extremely high risk they take. They could be seeking a return of 10 to 40 times their investment, over a time frame of five years. The returns they want from each start-up funding may seem very high but an angel with a portfolio of start-up investments will see many fail and *their aggregate holding may in the end return 20–30 per cent.* Studies of large numbers of start-up investments have shown that angel investors earn an average of 2.5 times return of the amount they invested over an average timeline of 3.6 years – that's a yearly return of about 25 per cent (Zipfel, 2016). Government incentives to invest in start-ups can be significant. In the UK, the Enterprise Investment Scheme can offer tax relief of 30 per cent on income and capital gains on investments from £500 to £1 million. The Seed Enterprise Investment Scheme allows angels to invest up to £100,000 across companies and get a 50 per cent tax relief. In Australia, investors get a tax offset of 20 per cent and capital gains exemptions. In the US, different states offer different incentives. For instance, Minnesota has an Angel Tax Credit of 25 per cent up to $125,000 open to residents of any country! Most countries support angel investors through tax breaks.

After funding by an angel, if your start-up continues to show potential and further funding is required, **venture capitalists** will probably be your next call. These are firms or funds that invest in start-ups with high growth potential in exchange for a portion of the ownership. Less than 1 per cent of start-ups get financed by professional venture capital firms. The reason is simply the high risk. On the other hand, half of venture capital funding goes to tech businesses. Early-stage venture capital investors look for high returns, given the high uncertainty surrounding the investments they make. They'd expect to get this through an **exit strategy**, such as another company or a private equity firm acquiring the business. This makes venture capital funding most suited to high-growth companies, possibly with proprietary technology, that are either fast becoming market leaders, and showing possibly a 30 per cent return rate. Lots of investors will look at an **initial public offering** (IPO), where shares are floated on the open market through an exchange.

Early-stage investors will usually want to claim a high stake of your business, because of the risk they're taking. So at the seed stage *you could be giving up 10–25 per cent of your company*. After seed capital infusion, the venture capitalist will fund **Series A** where you might give up *25–50 per cent*. They'll want to invest in a way that gives them some management control over the direction of the business. When it's clear that a start-up is doing well, but needs more capital, later-stage investors may step up. *Subsequent investors will accept lower returns*, because they're taking less risk. A business can go through many rounds of funding before finding and choosing an exit opportunity. So after the seed round comes Series A funding, followed by Series B, then C, and so on. With each round, a business can invest in further growth, and the risk usually drops each time. So at the pre-seed stage you'll own 100 per cent of your company. Then the angel reduces this to say 85 per cent. Post-series A you may find you retain 30 per cent and after the B round you could have 20 per cent left.

Where you get your venture funding from matters. The high-powered venture capital firms are called *Tier 1* venture funds (like Accel Partners, Benchmark Capital, Andreessen Horowitz and

Sequoia Capital). In 2009, Sequoia invested $8 million in WhatsApp for a 15 per cent share of the company. After further rounds Sequoia invested $60 million. This meant that when Facebook purchased WhatsApp for $19.8 billion in February 2014, Sequoia netted about $3 billion – a whopping fifty-fold return on its investment. But not all investments turn out this way. Many are duds. So venture capitalist funds have to be savvy and manage start-up investments very carefully. The fund might for instance have $200 million invested in 20–30 start-ups in a specific sector and may focus on specific financing rounds. There will be *general partners* who make investment decisions, undertake much of the research, engage in due diligence, agree terms and work with you in directing your start-up so it grows. They'll only put a small amount of money in the start-up if any. It is the *limited partners* who are individuals or firms (such as pension funds, hedge funds, endowments) who put up most of the money. For their effort, general partners will charge perhaps 2–2.5 per cent management fee (Startupxplore, 2017). They'll also take around 20 per cent of the profits made on the portfolio of start-up investments with the limited partners getting the rest. How much money you raise and how much of your company you give up is tied to what investors think it is worth. Let's turn to this now.

## Venture capital valuation

How do you decide how much of your company you should give up and how much money you should get in return? The maths is straightforward; giving up control of part of your start-up is more difficult. But, it could well make you quite rich, so it's worth considering properly. Suppose you launched a business six months ago. Your business now needs €600,000 from a venture capital investor who wants 25 per cent ownership. We'll call this Series A.

So, if €600,000 buys 25 per cent of the business, *the post-money valuation* is:

€ 600,000 / 0.25 = €2,400,000

Essentially:

$$\text{Post-money valuation} = \frac{\text{New cash input from investor}}{\text{Investor's required ownership}}$$

and the *pre-money valuation* is: €2,400,000 – €600,000 = €1,800,000.

That is:

$$\text{Pre-money valuation} = \text{Post-money valuation} - \text{New investment}$$

If the number of shares issued before the investment was 450,000, then the price per share would come to:

$$€1{,}800{,}000 \,/\, 450{,}000 = €4.00$$

Which just means:

$$\text{Share price} = \frac{\text{Pre-money valuation}}{\text{Pre-money shares}}$$

The number of shares to be issued for the investor is:

$$€600{,}000 \,/\, €4.00 = 150{,}000$$

So, there are now 600,000 shares: the 450,000 original shares plus the newly issued 150,000 shares. The founders have three-quarters of the total shares (75 per cent of 600,000) which is their *carried interest* or '*sweat equity*' valued at:

$$€2{,}400{,}000 \times 75\% = €1{,}800{,}000$$

Effectively:

$$\text{Carried interest} = \text{Post-money valuation} \times \text{Post-money ownership}$$

But, let's imagine that, six months earlier, an angel investor had put €16,000 into your start-up through a 20 per cent *convertible note.* In other words, the angel came in with seed money which was set up as a loan, and as the founder you agreed to pay the angel principal and interest on it. But, *the agreement also gave the angel the option to convert debt into equity*, if the start-up were to raise a round of venture capital or sell the business. This means that the convertible note converts into preferred shares when the Series A funding round closes. The *conversion discount* lets the angel investor convert the loan into shares at a price 20 per cent lower than what the Series A investor paid. Convertible notes are useful because, when getting seed money early on, it can be tricky to put a value on a start-up. *A convertible note enables funding without putting a figure on the start-up's initial value*, and means the angel investor gets certain assurances if the business does well. So, in our example, the angel gets to buy shares at a price of:

80% × €4 = €3.20 per share

meaning the angel gets €16,000 / €3.20 = 5,000 shares.

The angel gets ownership at €3.20 per share, while the Series A venture capital investor pays €4.00 per share. And remember, interest will have accrued on the loan, which can be used to buy extra shares at €3.20.

Sometimes, angel investors agree to a *valuation cap* as a way to reward them for the risk they've taken. For instance, in our example, a cap was set at €1,000,000. With the pre-money valuation of €1,800,000 calculated above, the angel would get the shares at a price of:

€1,000,000 / €1,800,000 = 0.56 × €4.00 = €2.22

That's quite a discount!

And from the money lent, aside from interest accrued, the angel would end up with:

€16,000 / €2.22 = 7,207 shares

The Series A investor would only have got €16,000 / €4 = 4,000 shares for the same investment. In this example, the conversion discount of 20 per cent is less favourable to the angel than the valuation cap (5,000 shares vs 7,207 shares). If the cap had been set at €1,600,000, then the angel would get a share price of:

€1,600,000 / €1,800,000 = 0.88 × €4.00 = €3.52

and end up with:

$$€16{,}000 \,/\, €3.52 = 4{,}545 \text{ shares}$$

Often, angels set up terms where a convertible note includes both a discount and a cap. The idea is that the conversion price can be set at whichever is lowest: the cap-based share price or the discount to Series A share price. This will maximize the angel's take. So, in our example, if the convertible note had been set at a 20 per cent discount with a €1.6 million cap, the note would convert at €3.20 per share (which is better as it is a lower price than the €3.52). The angel would end up with paper worth:

$$5{,}000 \text{ shares @ } €4.00 = €20{,}000$$

The 5,000 shares figure is just (€16,000 / €3.20) as calculated earlier. This is an unrealized return of 25 per cent on the €16,000, excluding accrued interest which would also be convertible at the €3.20 share price. Suppose the note was issued at 4 per cent interest. Then after six months, at the time of the Series A round, the accrued interest would be:

$$0.04 \times 0.5 \times €16{,}000 = €320$$

This could then be converted into 100 shares (€320 / €3.20). The angel investor would end up with 5,100 shares. If the Series A investor kept the requisite 25 per cent ownership stake, then after the round of financing, the angel investor and you would own 75 per cent of the company. As founder, your stake would be diluted as follows:

$$\frac{(450{,}000 \text{ shares} - 5{,}100 \text{ shares})}{450{,}000 \text{ shares}} \times 75\% = 74.15\%$$

There are other options for the angel investor. Instead of a discount or a cap, they might go for a convertible note with a *warrant* for a set amount. Say the €16,000 convertible debt had a 30 per cent warrant coverage. Then this would allow the angel to convert the debt of €16,000 at the €4 price (the Series A price):

$$€16{,}000 \,/\, €4 = 4{,}000 \text{ shares}$$

On top of that, they can exercise the warrant and buy a further 30 per cent at the same price:

$$€16,000 \times 30\% = €4,800$$

$$€4,800 / €4 = 1,200 \text{ shares}$$

This way, the angel ends up with 5,200 shares, and this dilutes your equity a little bit more.

If the angel plans from the start to convert their loan to equity, then you don't have to set it up as a traditional loan with a maturity date and interest. Instead, you can put together a '*Simple Agreement for Future Equity*' (SAFE for short). This isn't that different from a convertible debt – except that it isn't a debt! Instead, the angel expects their investment to be convertible to share ownership at a point you both agree to, but doesn't expect their input to be paid back. Of course, the SAFE can still have a cap or discount tied to it. Your angel might worry that later investors will get better terms than they did as a seed investor. If that happens, you can add a '*Most Favoured Nation*' clause to the convertible note. This will mean that the angel gets the same, or better, terms than later investors.

One issue about tech start-ups is that they often do not generate revenues for a long time while they continue to have significant funding needs. The *basic venture capital formula* is a technique developed by Harvard's Professor Sahlman (2009), to deal with the problem of *valuing start-ups which don't yet have any revenue*. It allows us to work out the pre-money valuation for such businesses. The idea is to work backwards from where the investor wants to be at a future point in time.

To see what this looks like, let's apply the basic venture capital formula approach to an example. Suppose that the average value for a tech company operating in your market space is two and a half times its revenues. A venture capital firm is looking to invest €2 million in your business. It expects that in five years, when it wants to exit its investment in your start-up, your revenues will be €60 million, net income will be €5 million and the price to earnings (P/E) ratio will be 15. They expect a twenty-five-fold return on investment.

The question will be: how many shares should be issued to the investor now and at what price?

Your start-up's post-money valuation is:

$$€60{,}000{,}000 / 25 = €2{,}400{,}000$$

After five years, the company is expected to be worth:

$$15 \times €5{,}000{,}000 = €75{,}000{,}000$$

That is:

$$\text{Value at exit} = \text{P/E ratio} \times \text{Net income at exit}$$

The venture capitalist will want the value of their investment in five years to be:

$$25 \times €2{,}000{,}000 = €50{,}000{,}000$$

At that time, their share of the business should be:

$$(€50{,}000{,}000 / €75{,}000{,}000) \times 100 = 66.6\%$$

In other words:

$$\text{Ownership at exit} = \frac{\text{Investment value at exit}}{\text{Value of business at exit}}$$

And as in the previous example, the post-money valuation is:

$$€2{,}000{,}000 / 0.66 = €3{,}030{,}303$$

And so, the pre-money valuation is:

$$€3{,}030{,}303 - €2{,}000{,}000 = €1{,}030{,}303$$

This remains the founder's carried interest.

And, if there are 500,000 shares outstanding pre-money, then post-money there should be:

$$500{,}000 / 0.33 = 1{,}515{,}151 \text{ shares}$$

That is:

$$\text{Total share post-money} = \frac{\text{Number of pre-money shares}}{(1 - \%\ \text{ownership given up})}$$

So, the venture capitalist will end up with:

$$1{,}515{,}151 - 500{,}000 = 1{,}015{,}151 \text{ shares}$$

And since

$$\text{Share price} = \frac{\text{New investment}}{\text{New shares}}$$

the shares are valued at:

$$€2{,}000{,}000 / 1{,}015{,}151 \text{ shares} = €1.97$$

It's very likely that if the company keeps growing, there'll be further investment rounds. The €2 million investment may not be the only funding requirement. Let's suppose that you expect another round of €1.5 million after two years, and another for €1 million in four years. There's going to be some dilution for early investors.

The investor in Series B will need the following share if it expects a ten-fold return:

$$((10 \times €1{,}500{,}000) / €75{,}000{,}000) \times 100 = 20\%$$

And the Series C investor will need the following share if it expects a five-fold return:

$$((5 \times €1{,}000{,}000) / €75{,}000{,}000) \times 100 = 6.66\%$$

So, after that, the Series A investor will have much less than their initial stake. That is: 100% less (20% + 6.66%) = 73.34%. The Series B investor's stake will also go down to 93.33% (100% less 6.66%) after the Series C round. If the Series A venture capitalist wants to keep two-thirds of the company, it will have to take dilution into account and make a bigger initial investment. The calculation for the existing ownership would be:

$$\frac{0.66}{0.7334} = 0.9$$

The required new shares number is:

$$\frac{0.9}{(1-0.9)} = 9 \times 500{,}000 \text{ existing shares} = 4{,}500{,}000 \text{ shares}$$

And the share price would be:

$$€2{,}000{,}000 / 4{,}500{,}000 \text{ shares} = €0.45$$

There would be 5,000,000 shares outstanding.

For the Series B investor, the existing ownership would be:

$$\frac{0.2}{0.9333} = 0.214$$

So, the required number of shares would be:

$$\frac{0.214}{(1-0.214)} = 0.27 \times 5{,}000{,}000 \text{ existing shares}$$
$$= 1{,}340{,}000 \text{ new shares}$$

And the share price would be:

$$\frac{€1{,}500{,}000}{1{,}340{,}000} = €1.12$$

Series C shares are:

$$\frac{0.066}{(1-0.066)} = 0.07 \times 6{,}340{,}000 \text{ existing shares}$$
$$= 443{,}801 \text{ new shares}$$

And the share price would be:

$$\frac{€1{,}000{,}000}{443{,}801} = €2.25$$

The total share number is 6,783,801 for an anticipated market value of €75,000,000. This equates to a price per share of €11.06. The yield for the Series A investor then has an expected return of €50,000,000 (allowing for rounding errors).

When a *liquidity event* takes place, venture capital investors expect a payoff. When they make their investment, investors will often identify a *liquidation preference*. Basically, this means certain shareholders will get preferential treatment when it comes to sharing out the liquidation proceeds, because of the risks they took at the start. For instance, suppose you and your closest friend, Rahul, are the founders of your start-up, with 40 per cent and 10 per cent ownership each respectively. The other 50 per cent stake is for your very smart venture capitalist who injected $400,000 into the venture. At the outset, the venture capitalist might have made their liquidity preference contractual in one of three ways:

(a) No liquidation preference attached to its 'A' shares.

(b) A 1 x liquidation preference.

(c) A 2 x liquidation preference.

Let's see what happens when we apply each of those three options to a liquidity event. We'll do the sums for a scenario where the outcome is a cash return of $400,000, vs another of $2,000,000.

Under arrangement (a) with a liquidity event payout of $400,000, the investor gets 50 per cent, so ends up with $200,000. Rahul gets $40,000 and you receive $160,000. If the payoff is $2,000,000 then your investor gets $1,000,000. Rahul gets $200,000 and you keep $800,000.

If (b) had been in place (the 1 x multiple), a payout of $400,000 means the investor gets the lot, as they invested $400,000 at the start; you and Rahul are left with nothing. But if the liquidity event brought in $2,000,000, then the investor gets back their $400,000 plus 50 per cent of the remaining balance of $1,600,000 – so ending up with $1,200,000. Rahul gets $160,000 (10 per cent of the $1,600,000) and you get $640,000.

If (c) was in effect, with a $400,000 payout, the investor again gets the lot. If the return is $2,000,000 then the investor would get 2 x $400,000 = $800,000, plus 50 per cent of the balance of $1,200,000, making their total payout $1,400,000. Rahul ends up with $120,000, leaving you with $480,000.

Multiple share preferences can heavily impact what you end up with. Best to remember: *what you agree to give up when you get funded has repercussions* – not just for this round but what you'll make in the future.

So, you're at the point where you've made your pitch, and impressed a business angel or a venture capitalist. You want to accept their financing. Now, you need to look at what you're getting into by entering a formal relationship with an investor. This means you'll need to ponder the terms and conditions on offer which, once accepted become legally binding. Let's take a close look.

## Term sheets: Look before you take the money

If someone very rich wanted to tie the knot with you, they may set out some terms and conditions and get you to sign a pre-nuptial agreement. If the relationship ends, this agreement helps determine what happens to your assets, income and wealth. In many ways, the *term sheet* is like a pre-nuptial agreement: it *sets out terms of the relationship with the investor and how you'll deal with the finances when it ends*. Unlike a marriage, though, investors will usually propose an alliance with the intention of ending the relationship – and soon! The term sheet outlines *the terms an angel or venture capitalist wants you to consider before they invest in your company*. It shows who will get how much money if the start-up eventually goes through an IPO, is acquired or merged into another company or, of course, undergoes liquidation. The key thing is that, while a term sheet can seem complex in its use of legalistic language, the more detail you have in it, the better. It's best to know about any issues of contention before you accept funding, rather than midway through. The term sheet allows you to negotiate terms until you're happy. And there will be plenty to think about.

Before you accept an offer of financing, some points should be high priorities on your list of what to negotiate. Usually term sheets will cover *three broad parts: funding, corporate governance and liquidation*. This is what you would expect. The investor wants you to know what they're investing, how they want to keep track of what you do, and of course, how they will get cash out of the business. You'll probably want to focus first on the value placed on your start-up. Most of us would want a high valuation. But, it could be that a lower valuation allows you more flexibility, with less interference from the investor in managing your start-up. So, don't just set out to maximize your valuation above all else. Take into consideration all the elements of the term sheet. For instance, one part of the term sheet could identify the need for a *stock option pool*. This is so you can recruit future employees by attracting them with share options. You'll need to address the question of how much of this pool should be 'pre-money' and how much 'post-money'. Make sure you understand if it's you who'll have to bear the brunt of the share dilution. Let's look at this more closely.

Say a venture capitalist will invest $1,000,000 for a 25 per cent stake in your company. This means the pre-money valuation of your firm is $3,000,000. The investor could then ask for a 20 per cent option pool that is fully diluted post-money. Basically, they want you to dilute your ownership to pay for attracting employees to the start-up. This would mean you giving up $800,000 (20 per cent of ($1,000,000 + $3,000,000) which is the post-money valuation) from your $3,000,000, making your real pre-money valuation $2,200,000. In other words, after the option pool financing and what you gave the venture capitalist, you'd have just 55 per cent ($2,200,000 / $4,000,000) of the company left in your pocket. The $1,000,000 investment effectively dilutes your stake down by 45 per cent, not 25 per cent, in this scenario. You'd be giving up 26.6 per cent ($800,000 / $3,000,000) of your share of the company, just so you can dilute your stake down to 55 per cent post-money! The investor is basically asking you to kick off with just 73.4 per cent of your company before you even take account of the dilution still to come. So, it's important to understand the effect of dilution on your ownership, and negotiate carefully. Also, bear in mind that, if you grow and go through further rounds of financing, *future investors will ask for similar cuts* now that this precedent has been set. After a few rounds like this, you may find you only own a small piece of the original pie. What's more, there will be other similar provisions in the term sheet that will affect your share of the business's value. Investors will probably *want you to vest your equity*. That is, they need to make sure you stay with the firm and retain high commitment. For this reason, it's important to have a vesting schedule for your founders' stock that works for you.

What you may prize most is running your start-up with flexibility and minimal interference. When you negotiate over the term sheet content, you'll need to understand what you're asked to give up, without the terms being too dilutive. Keep in mind that *how your board is structured and directors' voting rights* will affect how much control you have over managing your business. So, watch out for investors' provisions around the board's size, appointment criteria and your ability to appoint independent directors. Also, as we saw earlier, investors might try to build in multiple share preferences (see the previous example) when the business is sold. The higher this is set, the more dilution you'll suffer. Likewise, participation in the proceeds of a sell-out means you get a smaller piece of the pie. A '*cap*' may be in order. Ultimately, the more you give your investors, the less there is for you.

Your aim will always be to raise the most capital you can, ensuring you retain equitable decision rights and without giving away too much of the business you've built up. The investor's aim will be to maximize the return on their investment when they want to exit. You can see that your investor will ask for quite a bit in the term sheet to achieve this – so *negotiate until both your aims are aligned as much as possible*. Term sheets can be complicated to understand but it's really worth getting to grips with exactly what you're being offered and what you're asked to do. There are lots of examples of term sheets on the net. The one in the box below is a term sheet being offered to Susie and Uhuru, to meet their company BlueTech's financing needs:

**TERM SHEET**

Series A Preferred Stock Financing for BlueTech Inc ('Company') by Investix Inc ('Investor')

**INVESTMENT**

***Investor:***
Investix Inc.

***Company:***
BlueTech Inc.

***Founders:***
Susie D. and Uhuru K.

***The amount invested:***
$1,000,000 as Class A Preferred Shares ('Preferred') financing for BlueTech Inc ('Company') by Investix Inc ('Investor') at the Initial Price of $10 per share.

Pre-money valuation of $4,000,000. The investment will represent a 20 per cent shareholding for the Investor on a fully-diluted basis. The post-money valuation is $5,000,000. The pre- and post-funding capitalization of the Company is set out Appendix A.

***Dividends:***
8 per cent non-cumulative dividend preference as declared by the Board of Directors with pro rata participation in any Common Stock dividends.

**USE OF FUNDS**

The proceeds from the investment are to be used for:

**i** Working capital: $200,000

**ii** CAD machine: $500,000

**iii** Marketing: $300,000

**CONDITIONS OF INVESTMENT**

***Liquidation preference:***
The objective of the shareholders is to increase the value of the Company shares and realize this value through an Exit event. An initial public offering (IPO), a sale of the Company's shares, activities or assets, a merger, or a similar transaction will be treated as an Exit event.

Preferred will have the right to receive one times the Initial Price from proceeds on Exit with balance of proceeds paid to holders of Common Shares.

***Conversion:***
The Preferred may be converted at any time, at the option of the holder, into Common Shares. The conversion rate will initially be 1:1, subject to adjustments for stock splits, stock dividends, etc.

***Information rights:***
The Company will provide to each holder of Preferred (i) unaudited annual financial statements and (ii) unaudited quarterly financial statements and an annual business plan. This information to be made available with 25 working days from the end of each month. Investor will also receive annual audited financial reports from the company within four calendar months from the end of the financial year. These information rights will be valid until the Company's Exit or change of control.

***Protective provisions:***
Consent of majority of the outstanding Preferred will be required for (a) any alteration of the Articles of the Company if it affects the rights, preferences, privileges or powers of Preferred (b) any alteration of the number of directors or persons serving as directors(c) approval of a merger, asset sale, liquidation or other company restructuring or acquisition.

***Pre-emptive and Anti-dilution rights:***
The Investor will have a right of first refusal to purchase its pro rata share of any offering of new issues by the Company. This right will terminate immediately prior to the Company's IPO or Exit as approved by the Board of Directors.

***Co-sale rights:***
The Investor will have a right to tag along and sell shares with the Founders in the sale of shares to a Third Party whereby any offer should be made to the Investor on the same terms. If the Third Party has specified a maximum number of shares that can be purchased, then the Founders and Investor will be able to sell their pro rata share of the amount to be purchased by Third Party.

***Election of directors:***
Directors will be appointed to the Board such that (i) one director be designated by the Preferred (the 'Investor Nominee'); (ii) one director be designated by the Founders; and (iii) one director be designated by Common shareholders acceptable to the Investor Nominee and Founders.

***Option pool:***
The Company will reserve as the Employee Option Pool shares of its Common Stock the percentage shown in Appendix A below from fully-diluted capital stock following the issuance of its Series A Preferred which will be available for future issuances to directors, officers, employees and consultants.

***Founders matters:***
All intellectual property and other relevant rights are to be the full legal and unencumbered property of the Company.

***Vesting:***
All stock and stock equivalents issued will follow the following vesting schedule: 35 per cent to vest at the end of the first year following Preferred issuance. The remaining 65 per cent to vest quarterly over the next

three years. Upon termination of the employment of the stockholder, the Company will retain the option to repurchase at the lower of cost or the current fair market value any unvested shares held by such stockholder. Any outstanding Common Stock held by the Founders will follow the same vesting terms.

***Expenses and fees:***
The Company will bear its own fees and expenses and will pay counsel to Investors for legal fees and disbursements that are reasonable up to $20,000.

***Expiration date:***
These terms set here are valid until XXXX

***Binding terms and confidentiality:***
This term sheet and any related discussions and correspondence shall be held in absolute confidence by the Company and may not to be communicated to any party not related to the proposed funding. For a period of 30 days, the Company will not solicit investment funding from other parties.

**BlueTech Inc.** **Investix Inc**

Date and Signature Date and Signature

**Appendix A – Capitalization Table**

| Shareholder Name | Pre-issue Shares | Options | Preferred Shares Issued | Fully Diluted Shares | Fully Diluted Ownership % |
|---|---|---|---|---|---|
| Susie Founder1 | 500,000 | – | – | 500,000 | 35% |
| Uhuru Founder2 | 500,000 | – | – | 500,000 | 35% |
| Pre-issue Holdings | 1,000,000 | – | – | 1,000,000 | |
| Investors | – | – | 285,714 | 285,714 | 20% |
| Option pool | – | 142,857 | – | 142,857 | 10% |
| Post-issue Holdings | 1,000,000 | 142,857 | 285,714 | 1,428,571 | 100% |

You know your start-up better than anyone else. Venture capitalists can get it wrong… and live to regret it, as Marinova (2016) explains. Neill Brownstein of Bessemer Venture Partners passed on Apple, thinking its pre-IPO stock valuing the company at $60 million was 'outrageously expensive'. Ben Lerer of Lerer Ventures didn't pursue the Uber opportunity when he should have, noting later: 'I passed because I didn't trust my gut.' David Cowan, of Bessemer Venture Partners, said in 1999 to his partner who had rented out her garage to Google's co-founders when they wanted an introduction: 'Students? A new search engine? How can I get out of this house without going anywhere near your garage?' And here's what Cowan thought of eBay: 'Stamps? Coins? Comic books? You've GOT to be kidding. No-brainer – pass.' So don't be afraid to be bold!

## What about crowdfunding?

Crowdfunding is a way of *getting funding from a large number of individuals who each invest a small amount*. To do this, you effectively set up a campaign for your venture and tell the world about your idea, how much money you need to raise and by when. Many donors don't ask for anything back, or just want a minimal *acknowledgment* which makes *donation-based crowdfunding* suitable. This makes crowdfunding suitable, not just for business ventures, but for all sorts of projects that can claim to create value. While over two-thirds of campaigns don't meet their funding target, there have been lots of real successes in helping start-ups to raise funding through debt (from *debt crowdfunding*) or equity (from *equity crowdfunding*) or via rewards. It is a fast-growth industry with over 2,000 crowdfunding platforms available globally. More start-up funding comes from the crowdfunding industry than venture capital. The World Bank estimates that, between 2020 and 2025, crowdfunding globally will surpass the $90 billion mark (Crowdfunder.com, 2016). Others predict even faster growth (PIN Blog, 2016).

Debt crowdfunding or *peer-to-peer (P2P) lending* lets investors give money to businesses, in the expectation that they'll get it back with interest. With *equity crowdfunding*, as the name suggests, investors get equity shares in the business. Examples of equity crowdfunding sites are Crowdcube, Fundable and Seedrs. This approach can work well for tech start-ups with campaigns lasting for several months and funding being $100,000 or more. *Rewards-based* crowdfunders include Kickstarter, Indiegogo, Derev, FundRazr, Justgiving and Booomerang. With these you don't give investors a share of the business but instead just as the name suggests – rewards. If a start-up hits their money-raising target, the site will charge a fee of around 5 per cent, and the payment processor another 3–5 per cent. There are now over a thousand crowdfunding platforms, with variations across their models, industry categories and countries. Some sites offer a way to rate and sift through the crowdfunding platforms (eg Crowdfunding.com, CrowdsUnite.com, crowd101.com).

Obviously, when we're appealing to the general public to invest, there has to be some regulation. And as is often the case, the *systems for regulating business investments tend to trail behind advances in technology*. Still, the regulations around crowdfunding do try to make it easy rather than difficult to use this method, since regulators are aware of policies to promote entrepreneurship. For example, the European Commission sees crowdfunding as 'an important source of non-bank financing in support of job creation, economic growth and competitiveness' (Wardrop and Ziegler, 2016). In the US, the Jumpstart Our Business Start-ups (JOBS) Act also encourages and facilitates the funding of small businesses. The JOBS Act sets parameters on the amount that can be raised through crowdfunding. This is meant to enhance funding possibilities for entrepreneurs while protecting investors. The UK is also at the forefront of bespoke regulation for crowdfunding. The Financial Control Authority has issued rules around investment and loan-based crowdfunding which enhance opportunities for start-ups but protect investors – especially those without high net worth or who don't understand the risks.

There are some real pluses to crowdfunding. Aside from raising funds relatively fast, it can help *create brand awareness* for your venture, and lets you *test the market* for your product concept. If you have a great idea that just doesn't get any traction with conventional investors, crowdfunding could be the crowd-pleaser you want. What's more, having lots of investors supporting your idea makes them fantastic marketers for your product. And these investors are not after gaining control of you company. You also pretty much set your valuation for your company. Crowdfunding is no doubt a growing source of money for start-ups. Some thought is required though. Naturally, telling the world about your idea might be something you want to avoid as a start-up founder. You might need to sort out a patent, secure copyright or protect a design first. Also, failing to reach a crowdfunding target might dent your reputation, particularly for the people who pledged you money. There could be *extensive due diligence* since you're inviting the general public to invest and so the government has to have tight regulations in place for their protection. A lot of documents will be required to get ready (legal disclosures, filing statements, financials, etc) and these cost money. They often need to be lodged before you know whether you'll be successful in raising capital. You might well spend $30,000 plus on all this (Prive, 2016). And then you'll have to pay the platform its dues. Of course, the *reporting continues after a successful raise*. And if you need to raise more than the maximum allowed per year then that will prove very problematic (Title III of the JOBS Act sets the limit at $1 million per year). Careful how you tread.

## Summary of chapter

We've looked at:

- how equity financing could solve your funding challenge;
- the different ways to structure equity financing and what you keep;
- why understanding valuation and dilution is crucial for now and for later;
- the term sheet – look very closely!
- how crowdfunding works and why you must assess the benefits and costs.

## Review questions

1. Aside from the money, what's valuable about a business angel?
2. Describe three drawbacks of equity funding.
3. Explain how your start-up's future revenues tell you its value today.
4. If you were co-founder of BlueTech Inc, would you agree to the term sheet's terms and conditions?
5. What would stop you from using crowdfunding for your start-up?

## Further reading

Cunningham, WM (2017) *The JOBS Act: Crowdfunding guide for small businesses and start-ups*, Springer, Maryland

De Vries, H, Van Loon, M and Mol, S (2017) *Venture Capital Deal Terms: A guide to negotiating and structuring venture capital*, HMS Media Vof

Feld, B and Mendelson, J (2016) *Venture Deals: Be smarter than your lawyer and venture capitalist*, Wiley, New Jersey

Rich, JR (2014) *The Crowd Funding Services Handbook: Raising the money you need to fund your business, project, or invention*, John Wiley & Sons, New Jersey

## References

Crowdfunder.com (2016) Trends show crowdfunding to surpass VC in 2016, available from https://blog.crowdfunder.com/trends-show-crowdfunding-to-surpass-vc-in-2016/ [accessed 21.3.17]

Jee, C (2017) How to become a tech investor: Tips and advice from angel investors in tech start-ups, available at www.techworld.com/careers/how-become-tech-investor-tips-advice-from-angel-investors-3653386/ [accessed 21.3.17]

Lane, R (2013) John Sculley just gave his most detailed account ever of how Steve Jobs got fired from Apple, available at www.forbes.com/sites/randalllane/2013/09/09/john-sculley-just-gave-his-most-detailed-account-ever-of-how-steve-jobs-got-fired-from-apple/#5d99782fc655 [accessed 21.3.17]

Marinova, P (2016) I passed on Tesla: VCs confess their biggest regrets, available at http://fortune.com/2016/10/06/uber-apple-snapchat-missed-deals/ [accessed 21.3.17]

PIN Blog (2016) The best crowdfunding platforms in Europe, available at http://blog.privateinvestmentsnetwork.com/the-best-crowdfunding-platforms-in-europe/ [accessed 21.3.17]

Prive, T (2016) Why equity crowdfunding could be dangerous for investors and entrepreneurs, available at http://fortune.com/2016/05/06/equity-crowdfunding-could-be-dangerous/ [accessed 21.3.17]

Sahlman, WA (revised 2009) The basic venture capital formula, Sahlman and Willis, HBS Industry Background Note 9-804-042

Solovic, S (2015) Thanks for everything, now get out! When founders get fired, available at https://www.entrepreneur.com/article/243476 [accessed 21.3.17]

Startupxplore (2017) How does a Venture Capital firm work?, available at https://startupxplore.com/en/blog/how-does-a-venture-capital-firm-work/ [accessed 21.3.17]

Teare, G and Glasner, J (2016) CrunchBase sees rise in average seed round in 2016, available at https://techcrunch.com/2016/09/07/crunchbase-sees-rise-in-average-seed-round-in-2016/ [accessed 21.3.17]

Wardrop, R and Ziegler, T (2016) A case of regulatory evolution: A review of the UK Financial Conduct Authority's approach to crowdfunding, available at www.crowdfundinsider.com/2016/07/88046-case-regulatory-evolution-review-uk-financial-conduct-authoritys-approach-crowdfunding/ [accessed 21.3.17]

Zipfel, J (2016) What returns do angel investors make?, available at http://startupfundingclub.com/what-returns-do-angel-investors-make [accessed 21.3.17]

# Tracking your start-up's growth 08

Now you've got your investor's monies, you'll need to focus on your costs, revenues, profits and investment returns. In this chapter, we'll look at a few financial management concepts to use in moving your start-up forward. Both you and your investors will expect the time, resources and money put into your business to yield some return. So we'll start by considering the all-important 'return on investment' metric. We'll then discuss how a basic costing approach can be very useful though sometimes we'll need to use 'activity accounting' to really drive profits. This comes in handy particularly when investing in technology and a growing product range starts your costs mushrooming. We'll find that it's important to know the cost of getting customers, and then figuring out their lifetime value for your start-up. You'll learn here how you can use all this information to gauge your strategy along the way, and decide on turning points and pivoting your business. Possibly, there may come a time when you decide to leave your successful start-up behind – what exit strategies are open? Finally, we'll end the chapter with the 'Start-up Tracker' which brings together all that we've discussed into a scorecard enabling you to assess your start-up's performance and progress. So, we'll cover the following:

- your return on investment concerns you and your investors;
- you need to cost your products and know when you go off-track;
- activity accounting could help you make more money;
- getting and keeping customers can be costly – what to monitor;
- what to do if you want out;
- tracking your start-up!

## Are your returns what they should be?

All investors seek returns on their investments. In Chapter 5 we looked at how you can use ratios to analyse your start-up's performance. Once you know what your investors want from you via the term sheet, you can use the *Return on Investment* (ROI) measure to assess performance. Angels and venture capitalists pay extreme attention to ROI. It *reveals how able you are to deliver a return, by showing the income yielded for the amount invested.* We can calculate it as follows:

Return on investment = Income / Investment

So, an investor will look at it from this perspective:

Return on investment = (Gains from investment – Cost of investment) / Cost of investment

As suggested in Chapter 7, we can assume that business angels are looking to make 20–30 per cent return on their portfolio of investments with many venture capital firms seeking to make no less than 30 per cent. But, what do investors mean when they stipulate a 25–30 per cent minimal hurdle rate of return? What they're referring to is the *internal rate of return* (IRR). This is the rate that discounts the future cash amounts resulting from an investment. It ensures that *the sum of the present values of these amounts are equal to the cash paid now to make the investment.* The formula looks like this:

$$\frac{CF_1}{(1+r)^1} + \frac{CF_2}{(1+r)^2} + \frac{CF_3}{(1+r)^3} + \ldots - \text{Initial investment} = 0$$

In the above, r is the IRR; $CF_1$ is the Period 1 net cash inflow; $CF_2$ is the Period 2 net cash inflow; $CF_3$ is the Period 3 net cash inflow, and so on.

Suppose you've secured $1,000,000 in funding. Table 8.1 shows what your investor wants.

**Table 8.1** What the investor wants

| Investment | | Return on Investment | | Return of Investment | Cash Flow |
|---|---|---|---|---|---|
| $1,000,000 | × | 30% = $300,000 | + | – $300,000 | $0 |
| $1,300,000 | × | 30% = $390,000 | + | – $390,000 | $0 |
| $1,690,000 | × | 30% = $507,000 | + | $1,690,000 | $2,197,000 |

While your venture capital investor expects to earn 30 per cent on average, they don't really want a cash payment at the end of each year. And since there's no cash to be paid out at the end of Years 1 or 2, they'll want the expected 30 per cent on these unpaid cash flows accruing from year to year, on a compounded basis. That is, the IRR is 30 per cent because the internal amount continues to gain 30 per cent on the investment made. So, an investment of $1,000,000 into your start-up today could be worth $2,197,000 in three years, as shown above.

But, we all know things don't always turn out as planned. For a venture capitalist, maybe one out of a hundred start-up investments will produce a fantastic twenty-fold return for them. And perhaps a quarter of their investments will give a ten-fold return. But almost three-quarters will produce negligible returns, if any. So, investors don't actually look for start-ups projecting that a $1,000,000 investment will turn into $2,197,000 after three years. *If they did, they wouldn't be around for very long*, because so many start-ups fail to deliver anything! The only way venture capitalists can make money is by investing in start-ups which expect to have *a 10x to 20x cash return*. They need to have picked one that achieves this, and a few (about a quarter of their total) that produce 2x to 3x returns. If the rest are duds, that brings their overall returns down. Across the board though, their investments will yield the 30 per cent required IRR.

So, where does that leave you? If you've been offered financing, your projected returns are probably in the ten-fold or more expectations range. If your investor is expecting 10 times their investment in three years, that would translate into an IRR of 115 per cent – that is, the annual ROI each year has to be 115 per cent, which after three years yields the ten-fold return. You'll need to keep checking you're still on target for this – because they will! To help you, you could look at the ROI in a different way. You could break up ROI into two other elements of your business: the *sales margin* (income/revenues) and the *investment turnover* (revenues/investment):

$$\text{ROI} = \text{Income} / \text{Revenues} \times \text{Revenues} / \text{Investment}$$

So, if your income is $1,725,000 on sales of $3,000,000 and your investment base is $1,500,000, then your sales margin will be 57.5 per cent and your investment turnover is 2. This would generate 115 per cent ROI which *you would have to sustain each year for three years*. More likely for a tech start-up, you might see lower levels of performance on income or sales early on but with a very fast acceleration after that to still yield the 115 per cent IRR over the three-year timeline. You can increase the income for each dollar of revenues and you can reduce the assets you use to make each dollar of revenues depending on your strategy. If you improve either, or preferably both, you'll speed up your increase in ROI. You'll need to *wear two hats: your management hat and your investment hat*. You'll manage operations by understanding what's affecting the ROI from your business perspective, while also driving through your investor's ROI requirements. Your investor will assess your business by looking at the IRR and the internally monitored indicators that make up ROI (revenues, costs and assets used), so you'll need to be on top of this.

## How does a tech firm cost its products?

If you're setting out to maximize ROI, one way to do this is by *decreasing the assets you use* to make revenues (that is increasing your investment turnover). At the same time, you'll want to *maximize profit per unit sale*, so that your sales margin is maximized. Both of these will drive up your ROI. But what is your unit profit? To work this out, *you need to know the unit cost for your products*, so that's what we're going to focus on now. For tech firms making physical products, there will probably be labour and material costs as well as overhead costs (that is the indirect costs and fixed expenses of running the business). It's usually pretty straightforward to trace the material and labour that goes into making each unit. *Overhead costs are more tricky*: sometimes, they haven't been incurred yet (eg an insurance bill that comes half-yearly), or it might be impossible to tie the cost down to individual units. This might be the case if you have information system costs, or have to take into account the depreciation on an automated machine which makes a variety of products.

## Basic costing

Many businesses try to *allocate overhead costs for each unit by linking this with something that varies with production volume*, and which they already keep records for. This could be something like units produced, labour cost incurred, or machine hours worked. Let's look at an example.

Suppose a start-up in Nova Scotia, called Earmail.com, produces Bluetooth-enabled earphones. These read aloud e-mails from pre-selected senders into the earpiece, and the user can also voice a response. Earmail.com produces different sizes of earphones in two assembly departments, A and B. A is a bit labour-intensive, whereas B uses two robots. Earmail.com has worked out *budgeted overhead rates* so that it can allocate overhead costs to individual earphones. It uses a *standard rate, based on labour cost* incurred, to cover Department A's overheads. Since the main activity in Department B involves the use of robots, Earmail.com calculates a *standard, based on robot-hours*, to allocate the overhead costs for this department. By 'standard' we mean the budgeted cost that relates to one unit.

At the beginning of Year 1, Earmail.com made the following estimations (see Table 8.2).

**Table 8.2** Earmail.com: Resource usage estimations

| | Department A | Department B |
|---|---|---|
| Direct labour | $256,000 | |
| Robot-hours | | 40,000 |
| Factory overhead | $288,000 | $300,000 |
| Overhead rates | 112.5% of direct labour | $7.50 per robot-hour |

One of Earmail.com's product is the XL earphone whose costs need to be worked out. On 17 January, the costs for producing 20 units of XL earphones looked like this (see Table 8.3).

So, Earmail.com can figure out the unit cost for each XL, based on the standard overhead rates (112.5 per cent of direct labour in Department A and $7.50 per robot-hour in Department B) as follows (see Table 8.4).

**Table 8.3** Earmail.com: Production costs for 20 units of XL earphones

| | Department A | Department B |
|---|---|---|
| Materials | $40 | $80 |
| Direct labour cost | $64 | $42 |
| Robot-hours | | 26 |

**Table 8.4** Earmail.com: Total costs for 20 units of XL earphones

| Department A | | Department B | |
|---|---|---|---|
| Materials | $40.00 | Materials | $80.00 |
| Direct labour | $64.00 | Direct labour | $42.00 |
| Factory department overhead applied ($64 x 112.5%) | $72.00 | Factory department overhead applied (26 x $7.5) | $195.00 |
| Total | $176.00 | | $317.00 |

Total costs: $176.00 + $317.00 = $493.00
$493.00 / 20 units = $24.65 per unit

Earmail.com can work out the unit costs to include the actual material and actual labour costs incurred. But, it has to estimate the overhead costs using a percentage mark-up on the labour costs in Department A and the robot-hours in Department B. It collects information on both of these, since A is a labour-intensive department, and B is a capital-intensive department (the capital being the robots). This gives Earmail.com *a timely per unit cost amount*. But, as we know, they'll be estimating overhead costs based on budgets they prepared back at the start of the year. It could be that those estimates are a bit off by the end of the year. If this is the case, Earmail.com will have to adjust its accounts at year end for differences between actual amounts and estimated costing calculations for XL.

Still, for Earmail.com, the advantage of using estimates for overheads is obvious: it lets them come up with total costs (that are estimated) and therefore work out the product profitability. They'll use all this information to feed into and impact ROI calculations, as they must monitor all elements of ROI. *Timely estimates are often more useful than accurate information that comes late.* Also, if an estimate does turn out to be wrong, Earmail.com *will want to learn about what caused that discrepancy.* This is useful in itself for a start-up, as it says something about the sources of uncertainties. In the end of year accounts, you can adjust for any difference between the estimate and the actual amount of overhead without too much trouble. The source of the variances gives you useful information about market conditions, how well your start-up forecasts costs drivers, and any reasons for cost creeps.

## Watch those variances

Suppose that at the end of Year 1, Earmail.com finds that actual factory overhead cost is $320,000 in Department A (instead of $288,000) and $276,000 in Department B (instead of $300,000). They also find that the actual direct labour cost is $296,000 in Department A and the actual robot-hours are 36,000 in Department B. This means that *there were over-applied or under-applied overhead amounts (variances)* for each department, and for the assembly operations as a whole. Table 8.5 shows how to figure out the variances.

**Table 8.5** Earmail.com: Overheads applied

| | |
|---|---|
| Applied overhead (112.5% of $296,000) | $333,000 |
| Actual overhead | $320,000 |
| Over-applied overhead (*Department A*) | $13,000 |
| Applied overhead (36,000 x $7.50) | $270,000 |
| Actual overhead | $276,000 |
| Under-applied overhead (*Department B*) | $(6,000) |
| Total over-applied overhead (A + B) | $7,000 |

The variances meant that their cost calculations didn't quite match the actual amounts spent. Depending on what you use the costs for (for example, to price XL earphones, or to decide whether it's worth outsourcing some of the assembly), it can be important to get some accuracy over the rates. Earmail.com *should look at the variances continuously and see why they were there.* Knowing why variances turn up can be crucial when it comes to making good decisions.

As with any start-up, using cost estimates means there will probably be deviations from what we expect. Looking at variances can be really useful, because *they can tell us about when and how to pivot decisions and even strategies.* Start-ups should keep using information from its environment to decide when to alter its path of action. The cost system is a huge resource. A start-up can use it to continuously monitor for inflection points, and to search for signals that the existing operations might need to change in order to keep supporting the business hypothesis. And there are times when variances can tell us that we need to take another *look at the business model itself.* The estimates Earmail.com used for overhead costs can help the company to cost its production on a timely basis, rather than risk waiting too long for actual overhead costs. Earmail.com can also use its estimates to tell whether its understanding of the future is off-track. The size of variances also says something about how quickly the environment is changing. So, variances help start-ups reduce the risk of following a path for too long when it's time for a change. In that sense, working out that there's been a deviation from your plans isn't always a bad thing. *Variance analysis helps to give a start-up direction when the waters get choppy.*

But if we're comparing actual figures to budgeted ones for overhead costs, shouldn't we look at material and labour costs as well? This is, in fact, what firms do. They develop *standard costing* systems which use standards for all costs. These help firms to cost products well, to assess how parts of the business are performing, and to manage their risks. If deviations or variances from expectations are outside an acceptable range for a start-up, they can take this as a signal to follow a different course of action.

One reason for using standard costs is because they let us investigate what caused any deviations between what we expected and the outcome. If the actual profit for a start-up is not what we planned, the difference will depend on how far sales and costs have deviated from expected values. This raises the question of how much we should rely on the cash budget to work out our financing needs. To do a good job of predicting your funding needs, *you need to understand the sources of variances*. It's useful to look at, for example, the variance between the sales you expected and the actual sales activity. You might find that you make a plan, but the volume of sales you had predicted doesn't come through. You can't afford to be static in your thinking. You want to develop what we refer to as a '*flexible*' budget rather than a '*static*' one. Let's look at an example. Suppose a Copenhagen-based start-up called Stilhed ApS makes tiny plugs which can be used to silence any mobile phone. One of its product is the iPhoneStilhed, which totally mutes alarms, alerts and apps on iPhones (which do not fully silence even when on 'silent'!). Suppose that, for October, the Stilhed ApS budgeted sales of 60,000 units at a selling price of DKK 20 each, and a variable cost of DKK 12 each. Actual sales, however, were only 56,000 units. Table 8.6 shows that income was DKK 64,000 less than budgeted.

We could just conclude that the reduced sales caused net income to go down by DKK 80,000. It seems that variable costs were DKK 20,000 less than expected, which at least helped to offset the reduced sales. However, this is misleading. The DKK 20,000 favourable variance reflects the actual costs for 56,000 units compared to the budgeted costs for 60,000 units. This isn't great, since costs should be lower if sales are lower! We kept the budget static at the 60,000-unit level even though we want to know what the variances are if we had set the budget at the actual 56,000-unit level. It would, in other words, *be more useful for Stilhed ApS to prepare a flexible budget*, showing total variable costs for 56,000 units rather than 60,000 units, at a variable cost per unit of DKK 12. This is illustrated in Table 8.7. There you can see that variable costs don't in fact show a variance of DKK 20,000 that is favourable, but DKK 28,000 that is unfavourable. Since the company only sold 56,000 units, variable costs should have been only DKK 672,000 (DKK 12 × 56,000 units). But in actual fact, they were more, coming in at DKK 700,000.

**Table 8.6** Stilhed ApS: Budgeted vs actual income statement and variances for the month ended 31 October for iPhoneStilhed

| | Budget (60,000 units) | Actual (56,000 units) | Variance |
|---|---|---|---|
| Sales | DKK 1,200,000 | DKK 1,120,000 | DKK 80,000 U |
| Variable costs | DKK 720,000 | DKK 700,000 | DKK 20,000 F |
| Contribution margin | DKK 480,000 | DKK 420,000 | DKK 60,000 U |
| Fixed costs | DKK 100,000 | DKK 104,000 | DKK 4,000 U |
| Net income | DKK 380,000 | DKK 316,000 | DKK 64,000 U |

**NOTE** F = favourable U = unfavourable

**Table 8.7** Stilhed ApS: Income statement for the month ended 31 October for iPhoneStilhed

| | Budget (56,000 units) | Actual (56,000 units) | Variance |
|---|---|---|---|
| Sales | DKK 1,120,000 | DKK 1,120,000 | – |
| Variable costs | DKK 672,000 | DKK 700,000 | DKK 28,000 U |
| Contribution margin | DKK 448,000 | DKK 420,000 | DKK 28,000 U |
| Fixed costs | DKK 100,000 | DKK 104,000 | DKK 4,000 U |
| Net income | DKK 348,000 | DKK 316,000 | DKK 32,000 U |

The fixed cost variance is also DKK 4,000, which is unfavourable. Notice that the budget for fixed costs is DKK 100,000 in both the 'static' budget (for 60,000 units) and the 'flexible' budget (for 56,000 units). This is because, as we saw in Chapter 3, fixed costs don't change within a *relevant range* and both 60,000 and 56,000 are in the relevant range. That is, if we assume a relevant range of 0–100,000 units for Stilhed ApS's fixed costs, then these costs should be the same for both 56,000 units and 60,000 units of sales since the scalability extends from zero units to 100,000. So, within the relevant range, the flexible budget shows the same amount of fixed costs. However, if we go outside the relevant range, the flexible budget would show different levels of fixed costs. If we did a detailed analysis of the specific items of fixed cost, we would find the specific costs that led to the DKK 4,000 unfavourable variance. This would give Stilhed ApS good information about what overhead items they're not anticipating properly.

We can see that the actual net income was DKK 64,000 less than budgeted net income. Out of that, DKK 32,000 of the difference was down to variances in costs. Broken down, that's because variable costs were DKK 28,000 more than they should have been for 56,000 units, and fixed costs were DKK 4,000 more.

The fact that actual sales in units were less than budgeted also meant net income was less than expected. This difference is referred to as the *sales variance*. The sales variance (unfavourable) *shows us how much contribution margin we lost because we didn't achieve budgeted sales*:

Sales variance = (Actual unit sales – Budgeted unit sales) × Contribution margin per unit

Sales variance = (56,000 units – 60,000 units) × DKK 8 per unit
= – 4,000 units × DKK 8 per unit
= DKK 32,000 Unfavourable

The calculation above shows that, because sales were 4,000 units less than expected, net income was DKK 32,000 less than expected. This results in an unfavourable sales variance. The DKK 64,000 unfavourable variance in net income is as shown in Table 8.8.

**Table 8.8** Net income variance calculation

| | |
|---|---|
| Sales variance | DKK 32,000 U |
| Variable cost variances | DKK 28,000 U |
| Fixed cost variances | DKK 4,000 U |
| Net income variance | DKK 64,000 U |

So, all in all, Stilhed ApS failed to achieve its budgeted net income of DKK 380,000 on iPhoneStilhed plugs for three reasons:

- lost sales resulted in a DKK 32,000 decrease in expected net income;
- variable cost variances resulted in a DKK 28,000 decrease in expected net income; and
- fixed cost variances resulted in a DKK 4,000 decrease in expected net income.

Stilhed ApS should analyse these variances more, to find out the specific reasons for them. These will signal the need to change production processes and marketing efforts. They'll also tell us about how far the start-up is deviating from the investors' expectations. There may be environmental changes which get picked up when we look at variances, and this could even mean we need to alter the business model.

Suppose we have standards for material, labour and overhead costs for iPhoneStilhed plugs, as in Table 8.9.

For November, Stilhed ApS budgeted production for 24,000 iPhoneStilhed plugs. In the end, they only made 20,000 units. We can prepare a *performance report*, using a flexible budget of 20,000 units, as shown in Table 8.10. The budgeted amounts in the performance report are based on the standard variable costs per unit, multiplied by 20,000 units. The performance report shows that the total variable cost variance for November was unfavourable by DKK 18,444.

**Table 8.9** Total standard variable cost per unit calculation

| | Unit Cost |
|---|---|
| Direct material (5g per unit at DKK 1.4 per g) | DKK 7.00 |
| Direct labour (0.5 hrs per unit at DKK 16 per hr) | DKK 8.00 |
| Factory overhead (0.5 labour hrs per unit at DKK 8 per labour hr) | DKK 4.00 |
| Total standard variable cost per unit | DKK 19.00 |

**Table 8.10** iPhoneStilhed: Performance report for the month ended 30 November

| | Budget | Actual | Variance |
|---|---|---|---|
| Direct material | DKK 140,000 | DKK 134,964 | DKK 5,036 F |
| Direct labour | DKK 160,000 | DKK 173,880 | DKK 13,880 U |
| Variable factory overhead | DKK 80,000 | DKK 89,600 | DKK 9,600 U |
| Totals | DKK 380,000 | DKK 398,444 | DKK 18,444 U |

Let's look at how we can use standard costs to analyse variances. Suppose that Stilhed ApS wants to allocate variable overhead costs, based on direct labour hours. The following box shows the calculations we have to do to get variance values. The actual material and labour costs, and quantities used, are already recorded by Stilhed ApS.

## Stilhed ApS calculations of variance values

**Material price variance**

(Actual Quantity × Actual Price) – (Actual Quantity × Standard Price)
(AQ × AP) – (AQ × SP)
(97.8 kg × DKK 1.38/g) – (97.8 kg × DKK 1.4/g) = DKK 1,956 F

**Material usage variance**

(Actual Quantity × Standard Price) – (Standard Quantity Allowed for flexible budget × Standard Price)
(AQ × SP) – (SQA × SP)
(97.8 kg × DKK 1.4/g) – (100 kg × DKK 1.4/g) = DKK 3080 F

**Labour rate variance**

(Actual Hours × Actual Rate) – (Actual Hours × Standard Rate)
(AH × AR) – (AH × SR)
(10,800 hrs × DKK 16.1) – (10,800 hrs × DKK 16) = DKK 1,080 U

**Labour efficiency variance**

(Actual Hours × Standard Rate) – (Standard Hours Allowed for flexible budget × Standard Rate)
(AH × SR) × (SHA × SR)
(10,800 hrs × DKK 16) – (10,000 hrs × DKK 16) = DKK 12,800 U

**Overhead spending variance**

Actual Cost incurred – (Actual Hours × Standard Rate)
Actual Cost – (AH × SR)
DKK 89,600 – (10,800 hrs × DKK 8) = DKK 3,200 U

*(continued)*

*(Continued)*

**Overhead efficiency variance**

(Actual Hours × Standard Rate) – (Standard Hours Allowed for flexible budget × Standard Rate)
(AH × SR) – (SHA × SR)
(10,800 hrs × DKK 8) – (10,000 hrs × DKK 8) = DKK 6,400 U

Individual variances will tell us how efficiently and effectively Stilhed ApS uses its resources. But, as we saw above, we should also analyse the root causes of variances. This will allow us to gauge the uncertainty in the environment. You'll also be able to assess whether the business can learn from the past (including past mis-estimations) and apply this knowledge as you move it forward.

## Activity accounting

Tech start-ups offering a variety of products usually find that some of their services or products are simple to provide, whereas others are more complex. Also, they might sell high volumes of some products, and a lot less of other ones. These firms often find that the costs of producing and/or providing the service isn't just driven by the volume they supply. Rather, those costs can go up in a way that's tied to the complexity and diversity of the product range.

Imagine a firm with two products, which are both quite simple to make. It sells 700 units of one product, and 300 of the other. Then imagine another firm which also sells 700 units of a simple product. However, this firm also has 24 other quite complex products which each sell in quantities of 10 units, and a further 15 products that are really difficult to make, with sales of just 4 units per product. The overall costs will probably be much lower for the first business than for the second! Basically, the volume of production, or scale of service delivery, aren't the only sources of costs for a business. Complexity also has a cost. A business with a large number of products, some simple and some complex, will tend to have much higher costs than a firm making just one or a few simple products. Firms that diversify their product range and volume variety, find that costs rapidly grow to support all this diversification. So, *volume is not the only cost driver*. There are activities which drive costs and increase overhead costs, and which usually grow with product diversity and production complexity. This is especially true in tech businesses that frequently make product changes, as they respond to customer demands and evolving market conditions.

Let's look at an example to show how product costs can be distorted when a basic costing approach is used. Here, volume-based cost drivers will apply costs to products where we'll see there is variety, and the volumes of sales of each product differs. The Elppa Company makes four products: P1, P2, P3 and P4. Other costs are as follows: direct labour hour (DLH) cost = £10 per hour; direct material cost (DM) = £20 per ton; variable overhead (VOH) cost = £19,800; fixed overhead (FOH) cost = £40,920. The products have different selling prices and are produced in different batch sizes, as shown in Table 8.11.

Suppose Elppa Company uses direct labour hours to allocate overhead costs. It would calculate the overhead application rate like this:

$$\text{Overhead application rate} = \text{Total OH} / \text{Total DLH}$$

$$(£19{,}800 + £40{,}920) / [(20 \times 4) + (200 \times 4) + (20 \times 8) + (200 \times 8)]$$

$$= £23 / \text{DLH}$$

Now we can calculate costs for P1, P2, P3 and P4. Table 8.12 shows the calculated product costs and Table 8.13 identifies the profitability of each product.

**Table 8.11** Production data for Elppa Company

| Product | Selling Price (£) | Units per batch | DLH (per unit) | DM (tons per unit) |
|---|---|---|---|---|
| P1 | 350 | 20 | 4 | 5 |
| P2 | 240 | 200 | 4 | 5 |
| P3 | 550 | 20 | 8 | 10 |
| P4 | 460 | 200 | 8 | 10 |

**Table 8.12** Traditional costing for Elppa's products

| Product | DM | DL | FOH | Product Cost |
|---|---|---|---|---|
| P1 | (5 × £20) | (4 × £10) | (4 × £23) | £232 |
| P2 | (5 × £20) | (4 × £10) | (4 × £23) | £232 |
| P3 | (10 × £20) | (8 × £10) | (8 × £23) | £464 |
| P4 | (10 × £20) | (8 × £10) | (8 × £23) | £464 |

**Table 8.13** Elppa products: What are the profits?

| Product | Profits |
|---|---|
| P1 | £118 |
| P2 | £13 |
| P3 | £86 |
| P4 | –£4 |

Now, if we looked at the physical production process, we might see that the four products rely on different activities. The fixed overhead costs could relate to, say, two things: *setting up computers before production runs*, and *handling to deal with re-arrangements before the actual assembly*. We could see these set-ups and handlings as two key activities which drive the fixed overhead costs. We call this *activity-based costing*, since we use set-ups and handlings as activities *which take account, not just of scale, but of scope*, as the cost drivers for the two overhead cost pools (which make up the £40,920). Table 8.14 shows the relevant activity data that the start-up would have records on.

**Table 8.14** Activity-based costing data for Elppa

| Product | No. of set-ups per batch * | No. of handlings per batch ** |
|---|---|---|
| P1 | 2 | 2 |
| P2 | 6 | 4 |
| P3 | 2 | 2 |
| P4 | 6 | 4 |

**NOTE** *Total set-up costs = £16,368 **Total handling costs = £24,552

The cost drivers would be as follows:

DL + VOH = £10 + (£19,800 / 2,640 DLH) = £17.5 / DLH

Direct labour hours (DLH) is a volume-based cost driver, in that the more units Elppa Company produces, the more DLH it will need to use. The 2,640 DLH is the same denominator we had earlier: [(20 × 4) + (200 × 4) + (20 × 8) + (200 × 8)].

And then:

Set-up cost = £16,368 / 16 = £1,023

Handling cost = £24,552 / 12 = £2,046

*Set-up costs and handling costs are both activity-based cost drivers*, since each activity is needed for production, but the cost of each doesn't go up if we produce more units per batch. The batches drive the costs, not the volume of units within those batches for these two costs. Table 8.15 shows the activity-based cost calculations for Elppa's four products, and Table 8.16 shows the profit from each product.

**Table 8.15** ABC costings for Elppa

| Product | DM | DL + VOH | Set-ups | Handling | Product Cost |
|---|---|---|---|---|---|
| P1 | (5 × £20) | (4 × £17.5) | (2 × £1,023 / 20) | (2 × £2,046 / 20) | £476.90 |
| P2 | (5 × £20) | (4 × £17.5) | (6 × £1,023 / 200) | (4 × £2,046 / 200) | £241.61 |
| P3 | (10 × £20) | (8 × £17.5) | (2 × £1,023 / 20) | (2 × £2,046 / 20) | £646.90 |
| P4 | (10 × £20) | (8 × £17.5) | (6 × £1,023 / 200) | (4 × £2,046 / 200) | £411.61 |

**Table 8.16** Elppa: What are the profits really?

| Product | Profits |
|---|---|
| P1 | –£126.90 |
| P2 | £3.39 |
| P3 | –£96.90 |
| P4 | £48.39 |

You can see that the profitability rankings have now changed, compared with the previous simple product cost calculations. If we assumed that only volume of production drives costs, we'd get our profitability ranking of the four products wrong, as it would seem to be: P1, P3, P2, P4. If, instead, we recognize that the set-ups and handlings relate to batches rather than the total volume of the products – that is, we recognize activity-based costs – then the ranking is: P4, P2, P3, P1. This is, of course, the exact reverse. If Elppa Company relied on the previous costs, it might decide to drop P4 from the range as it produces losses, especially if there were no strategic reasons to keep it. And the company would see P1 and P3 (the low-volume products) as being the most profitable. *Under activity-based costing, these are actually the least profitable products. We see that, in fact, P1 and P3 are loss-making, and P4 makes the most profit!*

An activity-based costing approach can help you make better decisions about which products to drop and which to carry, as it won't distort your figures on actual profits made. Confusion can arise when complexity, rather than volume of production, drives costs. This is *often the case where a tech start-up has to keep altering its offering, experimenting with new products while keeping standard ones that sell well.* If your start-up has little product variety and the resources to deliver the products or services or the users or customers can't be differentiated through drivers that relate to scope, then *a basic costing system should serve just fine.* But often, tech start-ups will have invested in flexible technologies, so that they can make different products in small or large batches. Here, it's important to remember that it's not just volume of production driving costs. *Without activity-based costing, a start-up might well report lower profits for simple products*, because the costing approach makes it seem as though they consume more of the costs. These products will likely be the first to be ditched, as decisions on which products to cut are usually based on individual product profitability. Yet, it's often these simple products, made in large quantities, that offer real potential for contributing to profits. At the same time, other products that sell in lower volumes and are *complex to make, will appear to generate good profits* per unit; this despite them actually being more costly to make. These become the products the company keeps, and promotes. If this happens, then over a period of time, when you look at the bottom income statement line after the deduction of the total overhead costs, you'll start to see diminishing profits. These will eventually turn into losses.

The losses will reflect the fact that a small number of specialized complex products will be costing more to make than the cost calculations suggest. Because of this error, the company will have set prices too low for the complex units. The high-volume products, which seem to cost more than they actually do, are in reality generating profits and *cross-subsidizing* the complex products with lower sales. So, if a business gets the wrong signals from its costing approach and drops high-volume products in favour of low-volume complex ones, it *could be swapping profits for losses*. In the end, bad decisions about which products to drop will lead to dropping more products that should have stayed. A start-up can find itself floundering into a '*death spiral*'.

## Getting customers costs money!

Growth is key to assessing a start-up's health. Any metric that's going to be relevant for a start-up needs to show growth, perhaps on a week-to-week, or month-to-month, basis. If we look at revenue growth, we should see evidence of traction. And are revenues recurring? That is, are existing users returning and making more purchases? For instance, if you've got a subscription business model for your platform, are existing users renewing their subscription, and how many of them are doing this?

But what if your start-up is not generating cash through sales? It may just have cash from funding. Then a key question will be: *what is your burn rate*? In other words, is your average cash balance at the start of the month higher than it is at the end? Working out the **burn rate** will allow you to see how long your start-up will remain viable. Put another way, you can *figure out how long a runway you have*, before you need to take off without floundering for lack of cash. We looked at how to prepare a cash budget in Chapter 6, which will determine the runway we have and the stage at which we'll need further funding. Working this out, alongside an estimate of when you think you will achieve break-even, should be part of any start-up's ongoing self-examination. But if your start-up is not at a stage where it produces cash from sales then this need not be an issue. This is because to show evidence of value, and likelihood of future growth – sometimes explosive growth – a company doesn't need to be making profits – just yet. In its first 20 years, Amazon.com hardly made any profits at all. But still, investors continued to back the company. When it was generating cash from sales, one of Amazon's strategies was purposeful reinvestment: basically, ploughing the money it made back into the business, to ensure its growth. Likewise, after 11 years, Twitter still hopes it will become profitable, as does Spotify. Uber has lost money since it was started in 2009, but recently it was valued at $69 billion. So, what signals do tech companies have to communicate to convince investors to back them? It turns out there are a number of important metrics that indicate a start-up's health.

For a platform, *the number of users is clearly important*, but those users need to be *active*, and the number needs to be *growing*. This book may have many readers, but profits will arise from future not past sales! The number of active users is an important metric that tells us something about growth. *If active users are falling, then a company needs to do something to stop this fall*, or it won't survive. If active users are growing, this is a good sign. Essentially, the cost of providing products isn't the only cost you need to worry about for a tech start-up. You need users, and getting them will also cost you. Businesses try very hard to get customers – especially loyal ones. Have you ever been really cautious about using a company's services, but after you did, found you used it from then on as your first port of call? All businesses try to maximize their earnings by getting, and keeping customers. *The first sale isn't always all that profitable, because it costs money to lure the customer in.* But, loyal customers offer good prospects for higher profits in the long term, because those initial costs don't pop up again. And loyal customers may persuade others to buy from the same source.

How far should your start-up strive to get customers? And how much does it matter to the start-up and its investors? In Chapter 3, we looked at the high contribution margins that tech firms can extract from products. We saw how this can lead to pricing that is focused on growing fast, rather than achieving profitability right away. Getting customers through your door is important. It could be that your product users are not in fact your customers. In fact, *your business model may be to have customers who see your users as the product!* Here, we want to look at situations where your customer will deliver profits and we're going to focus on the costs of getting them. Let's look at *customer acquisition cost* (CAC).

For tech firms, it's quite easy to figure out the cost of getting a customer. Targeted web-based campaigns give very specific outcomes, and we can work out the financials quite precisely. This is because a marketing campaign on the internet can be very focused, and keeping track of specific customer behaviour is relatively straightforward. As you know, income equals revenues less costs. Looking at the profit potential of customers is no different. We know *we'll profit from a customer if they can produce more value than what we give up to get them.*

The first step, then, is to work out CAC as what we spend on getting the customers, divided by the number of them we've got. If we spent $10,000 to acquire 100 customers, then the CAC will be $10,000/100 = $100. Next, we'll want to compare this to the contribution margin that each customer yields (remember the contribution margin equals the sales price net of all variable costs). In Chapter 3, we saw that the contribution margin shoots through the start-up to cover fixed costs, then once they're covered, directly grows profits. So, we should work out the CAC and treat it as a final deduction from the contribution margin. Essentially, we're treating the CAC as a variable cost. But that's not the end of the story. Ideally, you don't want to attract a customer who just buys from you once; you want them to come back. If you have a CAC, and after that, the customer makes multiple purchases, then the CAC is *not a variable cost for every one of those purchases*. It really is a cost you need to pay just once, and then deduct from all the expected future earnings from that customer. This is where the concept of *Lifetime Value* (LTV) of a customer comes in (Gurley, 2012).

Let's say that your start-up www.properticker.com provides a subscription-based service. The site collates and sends subscribers customized real-time information regarding property sales, according to the registrations made at a national register of sales. The site instantly customizes information by area, property type and price brackets. This kind of information can be extremely useful to property investors, real estate agents, mortgage brokers, builders and removals firms.

The start-up incurs costs of £200,000 per month in **search engine optimization** (SEO) and gets itself 40,000 customers. So, the CAC is £200,000/40,000 = £5. If the contribution margin per customer is £12 per year and the expected average life span of customers is 5 years, then the LTV = (5 × £12) – £5 = £55. The ratio LTV/CAC *is another useful way of analysing how profitable your customers are, net of acquisition costs*. In this example, it would be £60/£5 = 12. You'd want this figure to come out above 1. The only times it should be lower than that is if you were going for a strategy of kick-starting growth to get to a tipping point, for instance, or if you had another profit stream which trumped the acquisition costs' negative effect on sales profits. If you're very focused on LTV calculations, you might work out the cost of your capital, say, from equity, debt and other sources, and then adjust for the time value of money. The formula for LTV would look like this:

$$\sum_{x=1}^{n} CMx \,/\, (1+CC)x - CAC$$

Here, CM = contribution margin; CC = cost of capital; x = year

So, if your cost of capital was 14 per cent, then for our example:

$$\sum_{x=1}^{5} £12x \,/\, (1.14)x - £5 = £37.21$$

This is less than the £55 we calculated just now as anticipated value. This is because money you get in future years is worth less than if it were in your pocket now (for a more detailed discussion see suggested further readings at the end of the chapter). Another thing a start-up has to be prepared for, is that CAC can actually increase as you get more users. This may seem counter-intuitive, but remember: some customer growth is organic, coming from word of mouth and other sources to do with your past and existing customer servicing. It's not just a result of your spending on CAC, supported by your marketing budget. As such, you need to be careful that you don't see all user growth as coming from your SEO activities (in this example). Past marketing costs may be fuelling some of your customer increases, so look carefully at CAC in relation to new, *rather than blended, customer growth figures*. Clearly CAC may well increase as your customer population base gets bigger. Also, don't forget to identify your CAC expenditures, so you can figure out which ones are working for you. For instance, you might spend money on pay-per-click advertising, as well as blogging activity. You need to have enough *information to assess which of these impacts customer growth, and how much.*

While it's always great to show customer growth, giving you a positive contribution margin, start-ups are *prone to loss of customer loyalty*. Metrics that look at the loss of customers are useful in deciding what action to take. Suppose that properticker.com had 1,320 paying customers at the start of the month, but ends the month with 1,227. That means it has a *customer churn rate* (CCR) of:

$$(1{,}320 - 1{,}227) / 1{,}320 = 7\%$$

We can put this in revenue terms. Say its revenues are £1.25 per month per customer. Then properticker.com's *monthly recurring revenue* (MRR) will have gone down. The calculation for the *revenue churn* is as follows, and it gives us the same number:

$$[(1{,}320 \times £1.25) - (1{,}227 \times £1.25)] / (1{,}320 \times £1.25) = 7\%$$

Knowing what causes and affects your churn is crucial. Your competition may be offering a better alternative, or perhaps you can't fulfil orders at the right level of quality. Maybe the service you provide is just losing value. Looking at your *average transaction value* (ATV) will give you good signals about how far your customers like your products and their willingness to spend more – or less. You can *link revenues per user to time periods* (say the average revenue per user per quarter) which also is a good sales tracking mechanism for some platforms (see Berkowski, 2014). Monitoring these alongside your CAC, LTV and churn rates will help guide your pivot decisions.

Monetizing your start-up is going to be essential in the end whatever your strategy. Getting big fast could take longer than you expect and your investors may get impatient if value isn't being generated. Some start-ups have successfully relied on delaying bringing in revenues but *those that produce income at the earliest are the ones that will likely attract funding faster*. The '*Tech Start-up Tracker*' at the end of this chapter provides you with a performance monitoring scorecard for your business. The metrics we discussed are identified as key ones to keep track of in terms of where they should be vs where they are now. You can fine-tune with further indicators that become *key performance indicators* (KPIs) for you and *point to meeting milestones which tally with the ROI targeted*. But equally important is to link the metrics and variances to decisions about altering your operations and perhaps, indicate a need to pivot the business hypothesis itself.

## Should you have an exit strategy?

When you get a term sheet from an investor, you can be pretty sure you're getting the money. You've already been engaged in operations, and now you can ramp these up. But the other reason you want to be successful in this funding round is so that you can get to the next round of financing and continue on your growth path. You need to anticipate your financing needs well in advance. A six-month runway is not a long time at all, and may well be the time when you want to get the next round assured. In the end, you might go through several stages of financing, and see your start-up grow extremely well. Very few businesses become *unicorns* (start-ups valued at over $1 billion) like Adyen, Hike, Airbnb and Xiaomi – at the time of writing there were under 200 (see CB Insights, nd) – but still, any growth is to be valued. As your start-up grows, you have choices. Do you want to stay small, or scale up and manage that growth? Do you want to sell to a larger company which has the right sales and marketing team? You don't need to decide on your exit strategy right at the very start. When you think about any life decision that will take effort, be it learning to dance, speaking a foreign language or developing an art collection, you don't start off thinking how you're going to get out.

We should see a start-up as a company that could enjoy fast growth with the right input, until it gets to a stage where it can scale up. How do you know when that is? One indicator is that *your sales are growing and become scalable.* This is especially so for tech start-ups, where the technology they've invested in allows them to scale up. For revenues to scale and profits to grow, *effective cash management is vital.* We looked at the cash budget in Chapter 6, and saw how we need to align the cost of financing with the riskiness of the business. When you've become expert at cash management, and grown both revenues and profits by managing resources and reshaping your product, this is when you will perceive the bigger potential of your company. When your customer growth is being powered by word of mouth; you get positive press reviews; your inventory goes down rapidly; you need more sales staff – these are the good signs. Your CAC might even go down, your ATV up and your LTV will extend. Ideally, your other KPIs also show solid performance, as captured in your Tech Start-up Tracker. This is when your business has reached *validation.* You know the cost of producing the product or service, and you're making the profit you need. At this stage, you can think about extending your infrastructure to capture more and more market volume. But scaling up, even when all the right signs are there, is not necessarily the right thing for you. You may have good reasons to be looking to exit. These could be personal reasons, or perhaps you're just itching to get started with a new venture. Perhaps you've had an offer you can't refuse. What are your options?

An IPO could be what you want, but it may still be too early for that. Many entrepreneurs make sure that larger companies know about their products/services, so that if they're looking for an acquisition at some point, they'll consider the start-up a potential target. A large company may be a *strategic buyer.* They might want your business because they have the marketing capacity, but not the products you've developed. Or, they might not be able to take advantage of fast-moving market opportunities, and your company could give them a head start with that. On the other hand, there are *financial buyers*. They might believe they can increase the value of your company fast by putting in more capital. Or, they might want to change the management, or add expertise, with a view to a future sale or IPO. Take, for instance, Andreessen and his group of private investors. As financial buyers, they purchased Skype from eBay for $1.9 billion in 2009. Eighteen months later, they sold the company to Microsoft for $8.5 billion. For Microsoft, the strategic buyer, Skype was attractive as it could be linked up with its other products (Windows Phone, Xbox, Exchange, SharePoint). It's always worth keeping in mind what differentiates you from your investors: although, like you, they want your start-up to create value, their plan is always to exit while yours may not be.

## Summary of chapter

We've looked at how:

- you align your investor's ROI concerns with your own business aims;
- you can cost your products and analyse variances;
- activity accounting can help your start-up maximize profits;
- to monitor customer acquisition costs, lifetime customer value and churn rate;
- to deploy the Tech Start-up Tracker to ensure you're heading in the right direction;
- to think through your exit strategy – if you want out.

# Tech Start-up Tracker

| METRIC | TARGET | ACTUAL | VARIANCE | ACTION |
|---|---|---|---|---|
| Product Cost | | | | |
| Sales | | | | |
| Variable Cost | | | | |
| Fixed Cost | | | | |
| CAC | | | | |
| LTV | | | | |
| CCR | | | | |
| MRR | | | | |
| ATV | | | | |
| ROI | | | | |
| IRR | | | | |

## Review questions

1. Describe how you would try to maximize your start-up's ROI.
2. How do you calculate the unit product cost for an order if you only have estimates of your overhead costs?
3. When do you not want to use activity-based costing?
4. What additional three metrics would you add to the Tech Start-up Tracker?
5. Why not an IPO for you?

## Further reading

Berk, J and DeMarzo, P (2014) *Corporate Finance*, Pearson, Harlow, UK

Bhimani, A, Horngren, C, Datar, S and Rajan, M (2015) *Management and Cost Accounting*, Pearson, Harlow, UK

Kruschwitz, L (2005) *Discounted Cash Flow: A theory of the valuation of firms*, Wiley, Chichester, UK

## References

Berkowski, G (2014) *How To Build a Billion Dollar App*, Piatkus, London, UK

CB Insights (nd) The unicorn list: Current private companies valued at $1b and above, available at www.cbinsights.com/research-unicorn-companies [accessed 10.6.17]

Gurley, B (2012) The Dangerous Seduction of the Lifetime Value (LTV) Formula, available from http://abovethecrowd.com/2012/09/04/the-dangerous-seduction-of-the-lifetime-value-ltv-formula/ [accessed 21.3.17]

# GLOSSARY

**Accelerator** An organization that offers diverse support services and funding pathways for start-ups.

**Advertising business model** Model that uses internet platforms to sell advertising.

**Angel investor** An individual providing capital for a business start-up, usually in exchange for convertible debt or ownership equity.

**Asset** An item of economic value owned by an individual or company.

**Balance sheet** Financial statement which captures in summary form a company's assets, liabilities and shareholders' equity at a particular point in time.

**Bootstrapping** Start-up financing from internal resources – usually the founders' personal income and savings and any internal cash flow.

**Break-even point** The point where total revenues match total costs and the income generated is zero.

**Brokerage** A model where a platform brings together buyers and sellers.

**Burn rate** The velocity at which a tech start-up uses up its capital to finance its operations, usually prior to having the capacity to generate its own positive cash flows.

**Business model** The premise on which a business will create and deliver value.

**Business risk** Uncertainty concerning the product, the technology or the market.

**Business-to-Business (B2B)** Companies that sell their products to other companies.

**Business-to-Consumer (B2C)** Companies that sell their products to consumers.

**Capital** Wealth in the form of cash or other assets owned by a person or company.

**Capital structure** A measure of funds supplied by the owners (equity) relative to the funds provided by creditors (debt).

**Contribution margin** A product's price less its variable costs.

**Cost** The amount paid or given up which may become an expense.

**Cost leadership** Low cost strategy to compete with other market incumbents.

**Customer-to-Customer (C2C)** Companies that provide a platform allowing customers or users to interact.

**Deep tech** Companies founded on a scientific discovery or significant tech innovation.

**Depreciation** Value by which an asset decreases over time due to use, wear and tear, or obsolescence.

**Differentiation** Strategy where a company's products or services are viewed as superior compared to those of the competition.

**Direct costs** Expenses which can be readily traced to activities.

**Due diligence** Measure undertaken by an investor to ensure the start-up aligns with the prescribed criteria for funding.

**E-commerce** Buying and selling of goods and services over a platform.

**Efficiency ratios** These allow analysis of how a company uses its assets and liabilities internally.

**Exit strategy** A structured plan to terminating an investment to maximize benefits.

**Expenditure** Payment of cash or cash-equivalent for goods or services which usually end up as assets, some of which will be expensed.

**Expense** Money spent or cost incurred in an organization's efforts to generate revenue.

**Experience-oriented crowd users** Business model emphasizing user experience, crowdsourcing and value obtained from platform data analysis.

**Financial risk** The way business funds itself and its cost structure affects the risks a start-up faces.

**Fintech** New financial industry that applies technology to improve financial activities.

**Fixed cost** Cost which remains constant over a relevant range of activity.

**Focus** Concentration of start-up resources for expansion into a narrow market or industry segment.

**Freemium** Business model with basic service provided free of charge while more advanced features are charged for.

**Generally Accepted Accounting Principles (GAAP)** The USA-based accounting rules and standards for financial reporting.

**Gig economy** A labour market where short-term work or freelance projects are prevalent.

**Growth share matrix** Planning approach developed by the Boston Consulting Group which considers a company's offerings to help decide those to support strategically.

**Hard science** Focus on a start-up making pure research commercial.

**Incubator** Structure to nurture start-ups during early period.

**Indirect costs** Expenses that are not directly traced to activities.

**Initial public offering (IPO)** Process by which a company first publicly sells shares on the open market.

**International Financial Reporting Standards (IFRS)** A group of accounting standards developed by the International Accounting Standards Board (IASB).

**Investment ratios** Measure which looks at invested amount to profit accrued.

**Lead generator model** A business model based on selling information about users to other companies.

**Liabilities** A company's financial debt or obligations from business operations.

**Liquidity ratios** Measure of a company capacity to meet its short-term debt obligations.

**Lock-in** Increasing user resistance to switch away from the product or service.

**Milestones** Targets usually set by investors such as customer volume, revenue growth, profit achieved, etc.

**Network effects** Where goods or services offered gain value as more consumers use it.

**Networks** Set of interconnections to enable the exchange of information or resources.

**Net worth** Value of non-financial and financial assets owned by an entity less the value of all its liabilities.

**Overhead cost** Expenses associated with business operations, some of which may not directly link to production or provision of products or services.

**Partnership** A business entity in which two or more co-owners contribute resources, share in profits and losses, and are individually liable for the business's actions.

**Pivot** When a start-up alters direction enlightened by prior learning.

**Platform** A business model for harnessing and capturing value usually benefitting from network effects.

**Price-per-user** This is the price paid per user when a company is acquired.

**Product–market fit** Extent to which the start-up is in a good market with a product that satisfies that market.

**Profit** A financial benefit realized when the revenues exceed the costs and taxes enabling operations.

**Profitability ratios** Measures that indicate how well a firm is performing in terms of its ability to generate profit.

**Relevant range** The range of units over which a cost function is assumed to hold.

**Reserves** Amount of resources required to meet future reinvestment, payments and/or emergency needs.

**Restrictive covenants** Any restrictions on past employees such as not to join a competitor or vying for the company's business or clients. Also used to signal restrictions on debt financing.

**Risk-averse** Quality of preferring less uncertainty of returns when two options offer the same overall expectation of profit.

**Runway** The length of time a company can stay in business before it needs more capital.

**Scaling up** The time when a start-up can increase investment into active growth because of clear evidence of traction and value creation.

**Search engine optimization (SEO)** Process of technically or organically attempting to increase chances of ranking highly in search results.

**Seed** The initial capital used when starting a business which can come from the founders' personal assets, friends or family, or other investors to meet initial operating expenses and before further investment rounds.

**Series A** A company's first significant round of venture capital financing.

**Sharing economy** Where assets or services are shared between private individuals, either free or for a fee because of preference to share or rent rather than buy.

**Stockholders' (shareholders') equity** Amount of capital a business obtains from shareholders, plus income generated by the operation of the business minus any dividends issued.

**Subscriptions** Where the consumer pays to access certain products or services.

**Sunk costs** A cost already incurred which cannot be recovered.

**Tech start-up** A new business that will deliver technology-based products and services in a novel way, or that will create novel and innovative technology-based solutions.

**Variable cost** Cost such as labour or material or overhead that alters with changes in the volume of production units.

**Variance report** A report which identifies differences between the planned or budgeted financial outcomes and the actual financial outcomes.

**Venture capitalist** Person or company that provides capital for new or expending start-ups.

# RESOURCES

The following is a limited but useful set of information sources for tech start-ups:

- https://www.sba.gov/
- https://www.score.org/resource/list-startup-resources
- https://www.uspto.gov/learning-and-resources/startup-resources
- http://europa.eu/youreurope/business/start-grow/start-ups/index_en.htm
- http://startupeuropeclub.eu/eu-funds-and-support/
- http://www.welcomeurope.com/european-subsidies-beneficiary-SMEs.html
- https://www.gov.uk/business-finance-support/start-up-loans-uk
- http://startupbritain.org/
- http://www.techcityuk.com/government-resources/
- www.startuploans.co.uk

The following sites provide information on incubators, accelerators and start-up spaces:

- http://www.seed-db.com/accelerators
- http://seedaccelerators.jedchristiansen.com/home/list-of-seed-accelerators
- https://hubblehq.com/blog/the-official-list-of-londons-business-accelerators-and-incubators
- http://entrepreneurhandbook.co.uk/business-accelerators/
- http://www.nesta.org.uk/
- https://secondhome.io/

Other resources:

- https://ec.europa.eu/digital-single-market/startup-europe
- http://www.europeandigitalforum.eu/
- http://unicornomy.com/
- http://startupeuropeclub.eu/
- http://startupeuropeweek.eu/
- https://digitalcityindex.eu/
- http://s3platform.jrc.ec.europa.eu/web-entrepreneurship-and-start-ups
- http://blog.ycombinator.com/how-to-raise-a-seed-round/
- http://www.investopedia.com/uk/
- https://blog.crowdfunder.com/crowdfunding-startups/crowdfunding-terms/

# INDEX

Note: chapter references and summaries are indexed as 'references' *and* 'chapter summaries'; 'further reading' and 'review questions' are indexed as such. Page numbers in *italics* indicate Figures or Tables.

CPSIA information can be obtained
at www.ICGtesting.com
Printed in the USA
BVOW10s0840241117
501093BV00004B/255/P